Building an Intelligence-Led Security Program

Building an Intelligence-Led Security Program

Allan Liska

Tim Gallo, Technical Editor

AMSTERDAM • BOSTON • HEIDELBERG • LONDON
NEW YORK • OXFORD • PARIS • SAN DIEGO
SAN FRANCISCO • SINGAPORE • SYDNEY • TOKYO
Syngress Publishers is an Imprint of Elsevier

SYNGRESS.

Acquiring Editor: Chris Katsaropoulos
Editorial Project Manager: Benjamin Rearick
Project Manager: Preethy Simon
Designer: Mark Rogers

Syngress is an imprint of Elsevier
225 Wyman Street, Waltham, MA 02451, USA

Library of Congress Cataloging-in-Publication Data
A catalog record for this book is available from the Library of Congress

British Library Cataloguing-in-Publication Data
A catalogue record for this book is available from the British Library

ISBN: 978-0-12-802145-3

For information on all Syngress publications
visit our website at store.elsevier.com/Syngress

Working together
to grow libraries in
developing countries

www.elsevier.com • www.bookaid.org

To Kris and Bruce, we lost a lot of time together while I was writing. I am excited to make that time up. I love you both and could not have finished without your support.

Contents

Introduction

In February of this year I was on the floor of the RSA conference, the first one I had been to in many years, and I was struck by how much security seems to have changed in a very short time. Actually, to be more accurate, I was struck by how much security *marketing* seems to have changed in a very short time.

Almost every security vendor at RSA was touting its intelligence, whether it was native intelligence provided by the vendor directly into its platform or the vendor's integration with third-party intelligence providers. Don't get me wrong, I am a firm believer that intelligence is the best way to identify and resolve security incidents before they become a problem. But intelligence is not a data feed or a series of indicators. Instead, intelligence is a process that takes those indicators, makes them actionable, and provides context around the threat behind those indicators.

In fact, it was a conversation on this topic with the technical editor for this book, Tim Gallo, on a very rainy night at RSA that lead to the development of this book. This book is not meant to be a purely technical book, in terms of configuring systems. Instead, the goal of the book is to help the reader determine how to adjust security processes within the organization to accommodate the intelligence cycle and to think about where the resulting intelligence can be injected. Better intelligence, used properly, leads to better protection of the network.

This is a first attempt to cover a complex topic, a version 1.0 if you will. I would greatly appreciate any feedback, positive or negative, you have – hopefully it will help make the next version even better. You can reach me at allan@allan.org with any comments and if you want to try to spear phish me your best bets are: DC and Marvel, red heads, and Bordeaux. Enjoy the book!

About the Author

Allan Liska is the director of the Technology Alliance Program at iSIGHT Partners and an "accidental" security expert. While Allan has always been good at breaking things, he got his start professionally working as a customer service representative at GEnie Online Services (a long defunct early competitor to AOL), where he would spend his off hours figuring out how users had gain unauthorized access to the system, booting them off, and letting the developers know what needed to be patched. Unknowingly, this was leading him down the path of becoming a security professional. Since then he has work at companies like UUNET and Symantec, helping companies better secure their networks. He has also worked at Boeing trying to break into those company networks. Today Allan helps companies operationalize intelligence – getting all of the security devices to talk to each other and adding an intelligence overlay.

In addition to his time spent on both sides of the security divide, Allan has written extensively on security including *The Practice of Network Security* and he was a contributing author to *Apache Administrator's Handbook*.

About the Technical Editor

Tim Gallo is a field engineer with Symantec; he has 11 years of experience at Symantec and 16 years of experience in information technology and IT security. As field engineer for Symantec's Cyber Security Group, he provides strategy and direction for Symantec's customers and their leveraging of intelligence collection and dissemination to create proactive protection schemes. He has served Symantec in other capacities including: technical product management for Symantec's intelligence offerings, operational, and delivery roles within the Global Services and Engineering teams, as well as leading the company's advanced networks security products support strategies. Tim joined Symantec after holding the role of America's security officer for a leading industrial manufacturer where he was responsible for strategic policy development, testing, and data-center operations. As a part of his current role, Tim provides thought leadership in the areas of security strategy, intelligence initiatives, and threat and vulnerability management. Tim also likes wines, craft beers, lock-picking and riding his Harley along the coasts.

Acknowledgments

An overarching theme of this book is the importance of information sharing. Intelligence is useless unless it is actionable and in the hands of the person who needs it in time for that person to act on it. This book would not be possible without the willingness of so many people in the cyber threat intelligence community to share their knowledge with me.

There are a number of people I want to give special thanks to for their help: Brian Tillett at Cisco, Ben Johnson and Jeffrey Guy at Carbon Black, Mike Cryer and Scott Fuselier at CrowdStrike, Geoff Stowe at Palantir, Sean Murphy at Symantec, Justin Bajko at Mandiant, Jason Hines at Recorded Future, Tim Chen at DomainTools, Laura Schweitzer at Schweitzer Engineering Laboratories, Patrick Clancy at Reservoir Labs, Chris Goodwin and Chris Caldwell at LockPath, Andy Pendergast and Michele Perry at ThreatConnect, Sean Blenkhorn at eSentire, and Wayne Chiang at ThreatQuotient.

I also want to thank my coworkers at iSIGHT Partners for all of the support you have given me during this period. Your support, advice, thoughts, and access allowed me to write a book that will be truly helpful to a wide audience.

In addition to the wide community support I also want to thank Tim Gallo for his excellent work as technical editor. Given the countless hours Tim and I have spent honing our thoughts on the effective use of cyber threat intelligence within an organization this book is as much his at is mine. In fact, some of the smartest passages in this book are directly taken from his edits.

Finally, this book would not have happened without the hard work of Chris Katsaropoulos and Ben Rearick at Syngress. Chris thank you for believing in the idea and helping me mold my thoughts. Ben, thank you for keeping me (mostly) on schedule and for nudging me along when I got stuck. You both made this process a lot easier than it was 10 years ago.

Understanding the threat

1

INFORMATION IN THIS CHAPTER:

- A Brief History of Network Security
- Understanding the Current Threat
- The Coming Threats

INTRODUCTION

In 1981, the great Jon Postel wrote in RFC (request for comments) 793, "be conservative in what you do, be liberal in what you accept from others." Postel was introducing the Transmission Control Protocol (TCP) for the Defense Advanced Research Projects Agency (DARPA, 1981) Internet Program. TCP is what underpins the majority of Internet communication today, and it works because of that sentence, known today as Postel's Law. For network systems to be interoperable with each other they need to be forgiving about the traffic they accept but fully compliant with established protocols when sending out traffic. Postel's Law also demonstrates the mindset that was necessary in the early development of the Internet. Because Internet communication was relatively new it needed to be as open and accessible as possible.

It is that openness that led to the rise of the Internet, to the point today that many users and organizations consider it indispensable to their daily living. Unfortunately, that openness also means that the systems connected to the Internet are susceptible to attack.

It is the nature and evolution of these attacks that is the focus of this chapter. It is impossible to understand how to protect against today's and tomorrow's attacks without first understanding where these attacks come from and how they have morphed over the years from scientific research to fame seekers to multibillion-dollar businesses. As threats continue to evolve, so must the solution to those threats.

A BRIEF OF HISTORY OF NETWORK SECURITY

Any discussion of using intelligence to improve network security must begin with an understanding of the history of network security. After all, without an understanding of the past and how security threats have evolved it would be difficult to understand where the future of network security is headed.

Depending on who is asked what is known as the Internet today started in 1982 with the release of the Transmission Control Protocol/Internet Protocol (TCP/IP) by the Defense Information Systems Agency (DISA) and the Advanced Research Projects Agency (ARPA). According to Hobbes' Internet Timeline (Zakon, 2014), this was the first time that the word "internet" was used to define a set of connected networks.

At this point in time the Internet was very small, consisting primarily of universities and government agencies, and very open. To access another node on the network operators had to share address information. Each operator was responsible for maintaining a table of all the nodes on the Internet and updates were sent out when things changed.

THE MORRIS WORM

A lot of that openness changed on November 2, 1988 with the release of the Morris Worm (Seltzer, 2013). There had been security breaches prior to the Morris Worm, but the Morris Worm focused attention of the fledging network on security.

Ostensibly built to conduct a census of the nodes on the Internet, the Morris Worm wound up knocking an estimated 10% of the fledgling Internet offline (6000 of an estimated 60,000 nodes). The Morris Worm used a number of tricks still in use by worm creators today, including redirection (Morris was at Cornell but launched the worm from the Massachusetts Institute of Technology [MIT]), password guessing, automated population, and the use of a buffer overflow attack.

Good intentions or not, the Morris Worm clearly was designed to gain unauthorized access to nodes on the Internet and to bypass what little security was in place. The Morris Worm led directly to the founding of the CERT Coordination Center (CERT/CC) at Carnegie Mellon University, an organization that still exists today. The Morris Worm also pushed the development of the firewall as the first network security measure.

FIREWALLS

Like many terms used to describe network protocols, firewall is a term taken from the physical world. A firewall is a structure that is used to slow down or prevent a fire from spreading from one house to another or one part of a house to another part. Its purpose is to contain fire and limit damage to a single structure or part of that structure.

Most modern townhouses and condominiums have firewalls between adjacent units and firewalls can be even larger. The January 1911 edition of the *Brotherhood of Locomotive Firemen and Enginemen's Magazine* (p 90) describes a firewall erected in Manhattan stretching from 9th Street to 5th Avenue. This firewall was built to protect Manhattan from large-scale fires similar to what happened to Baltimore and San Francisco.

The earliest form of network firewall was developed in the late 1980s and was initially simply packet filtering rules added to routers. Packet filtering at the gateway level allowed network operators to stop known bad traffic from entering the network, but only provided limited improvements to security. These rules are difficult to maintain and very prone to false positives (blocking traffic that is actually good) and they require extensive knowledge of who everyone in the organization needs to talk to and who everyone needs to block. Packet filtering was ideal when the Internet consisted of 60,000 nodes and was considered very small, but it quickly outgrew its usefulness and new form firewall was needed.

The next type of firewall created was one that allowed for stateful packet filtering. These were the first commercial firewalls introduced by Digital Equipment Corporation (DEC) and AT&T. A stateful packet filtering firewall is one that maintains a table of all connections that pass through it. It makes its decision based not only the type of traffic but the status of the connection between the two hosts. A stateful packet filtering firewall is able to make more contextual-based decisions about whether traffic is good or bad based on the state of the packet. Stateful packet filtering firewalls were really the start of the commercial network security market. From this point firewall development enters a rapid pace and features like proxy capabilities, deep packet inspection, application awareness, and VPN (virtual private network) capabilities are added to firewalls.

INTRUSION DETECTION SYSTEMS

The problem with a firewall is that, for the most part, administrators must be aware of a threat in order to put a rule in that will block it. Now that is not always the case, even in the late 1990s there were firewalls, like the Raptor Firewall, that were able to assess traffic based upon published standards (e.g. the RFC standards for Secure Sockets Layer [SSL], Simple Mail Transfer Protocol [SMTP], Hypertext Transfer Protocol [HTTP], etc). The capability to monitor for protocol compliance puts them inline with the capabilities of some of today's "next-generation" firewalls. Unfortunately, most firewalls were not able to alert on rules that they did not know about, a problem that makes firewalls ineffective against unknown threats. To handle unknown threats most networks deploy an Intrusion Detection System (IDS). An IDS is useful for detecting threats either by traffic pattern (e.g. if a URL contains characters it is associated with Qakbot, a data-stealing malware virus) or anomalous activity (e.g. these are Alice's credentials, but Alice does not usually log into the VPN from Estonia).

There were a number of precursors to the IDS proposed in the 1980s, primarily to manage the auditing of log files, which until that point was manual process often involving printing out logs onto reams of paper each week and manually verifying them.

The first modern IDS, and one that underpins much of the way today's IDSs work, was proposed by Dorothy Denning in 1987 in a paper entitled *An Intrusion-Detection Model*.

The model Denning outlined in her paper was for an Intrusion-Detection Expert System (IDES), which had six main components:

1. Subjects
2. Objects
3. Audit Records
4. Profiles
5. Anomaly Records
6. Activity Rules

By combining understanding of who the users of the network are (subjects) with the resources those users are trying to access (objects) and the logs (audit records) from those resources the IDES was able to build a strong profile of who is on the network and what they are doing on that network.

Taking that first set of data the IDES operators were able to automatically build a table mapping out the general patterns of activity on the network (profiles) as well as any activity that fell outside of those patterns (anomaly records). This allowed network administrators to develop signatures that alert when behavior that is not expected occurs (activity rules).

Moving from the original IDES to the modern IDS, these solutions tend to be network centric, which means they have lost some of the depth proposed by the original IDES solution. The modern IDS is good, often very good, at detecting malicious network activity but not necessarily good at detecting malicious activity on the desktop, or anomalous activity. An IDS might see that Alice has emailed her client list to her gmail account, but it doesn't know that Alice just gave her notice. For many years the focus of the IDS and IDS developers was building better signatures and delivering those signatures faster, rather than focusing on building an understanding of the network and learning the context of the traffic. Fortunately, that is starting to change.

THE DESKTOP

In 1971 a programmer named Robert Thomas at BBN Technologies developed the first working computer virus (DNEWS, 2011) (the idea had been proposed as early as 1949). The virus, known as Creeper, was a self-replicating worm that jumped from one TENEX system to other TENEX time-sharing systems that were running on the DEC PDP-10 and connected to ARPANET. Ostensibly created as a research tool, the virus would start a print job, stop it and make the jump to another system removing itself from the original system. Once it installed on the new system it would print the message "I'M THE CREEPER. CATCH ME IF YOU CAN!" on the screen.

Coincidentally, Creeper led directly to the first antivirus program, the Reaper, which jumped from system to system removing the Creeper.

The first widespread virus created outside of the network was called Elk Cloner. Elk Rich Skrenta, a 15-year-old high school student, programmed Cloner in February 1982. Elk Cloner was a boot-sector virus that infected Apple II machines. When these machines booted from an infected floppy the virus was copied into the computer's memory and remained installed on the computer. In addition, any uninfected floppy that was inserted into the machine had the Elk Cloner worm copied to it, allowing it to spread from machine to machine via floppy.

The virus did not do much damage, but every fiftieth time the program it was attached to ran it would display the following program:

Elk Cloner: The program with a personality
It will get on all your disks
It will infiltrate your chips
Yes, it's Cloner!
It will stick to you like glue
It will modify RAM too
Send in the Cloner!

Of course, virus creation was just getting started. Throughout the 1980s new and innovative ways to spread infections were developed; some of those techniques are still used today. In 1983 the Trojan ARF-ARF was the first known virus that spread via Bulletin Board System (BBS) and in 1986 the Pakistani Flu, also known as the Brain virus, was the first to impact IBM PC–compatible computers.

According to most counts, between January 1982 and December 1990 an estimated 310 viruses were released into the world. Compare that to 2013 where Kaspersky Labs reported discovering 315,000 new malicious files each day, for a total of 114,975,000 just in 2013 (Kaspersky Labs, 2013).

In the 1980s and the early part of the 1990s most viruses were spread using floppy disks. Although there was some network-centric malware, most virus creators focused on spreading viruses via floppy disks. Even Trojan viruses downloaded from a BBS, if they spread at all, relied on the floppy disk to propagate.

To combat the rising threat of viruses and worms inside the network, organizations began installing antivirus software in the late 1980s. Of course, the concept of an antivirus program was not new in the late 1980s. In fact, the use of the term *virus* to describe a "…program that can 'infect' other programs by modifying them to include a possibly evolved copy of itself" was first coined by Fred Cohen in 1984 in a paper entitled *A Computer Virus* (Cohen, 1984). In the paper, Cohen outlined what constitutes a computer virus, effective methods for detecting those viruses, and suggestions for methods to remove those viruses. Presciently, the paper also states that "…prevention of computer viruses may be infeasible."

Cohen's work led directly to the development of the first commercial antivirus solutions, which were released in the late 1980s and early 1990s and are ubiquitous inside large and small networks today.

Early antivirus programs were largely based on signature detection, which was manageable when new malware was released at the rate of hundreds each year, rather than hundreds each minute. In addition to rapidly growing numbers, virus makers quickly learned to create polymorphic viruses. A polymorphic virus is one that modifies itself each time it is copied in order to avoid detection by antivirus programs.

Although the basic function of the code remains the same, the shell that encases the core functionality changes. This led antivirus makers to develop heuristic detection mechanisms that focused on the behavior of the code, not on the code itself.

Although most antivirus vendors still rely heavily on signature-based detection, almost all of them also look at the behavior of the code running on the machine and make decisions based on that behavior. This is especially critical now that most malware is only deployed on a handful of machines before it is morphed and the attacker goes on to the next set of victims.

THE MAIL FILTER AND THE PROXY

With the rise of the Internet, and the number of organizations connected to it, a new set of attacks was born. Spam, phishing, and malicious Web sites often overwhelmed resources and led to mass infections inside the network. It was no longer enough to monitor network traffic administrators also needed to have awareness of the content and context of that traffic.

In the new connected world, a network infection that started in one network with a macro embedded in a Microsoft Word document or Adobe PDF file could (and usually did) quickly and easily spread to other networks.

Of course, it wasn't just infected files that mail administrators had to worry about, spam and phishing also quickly grew into a big problem. At one point, spam accounted for almost 70% of all email (Gudkova, 2014). Even though spam was plentiful, it was also relatively easy to deal with from a security perspective. With the right tools, it was easy to quickly identify and keep most spam email from reaching users, while only producing a few false-positives that could be corrected by adding custom rules.

Phishing was, and continues to be, a very different problem. The term *phishing* was first used in 1996 on the Usenet Group alt.online-server.america.online (Phishing. org, n.d.) and the America Online Service was the first heavily targeted mail system by phishing attacks. A phishing email is distinct from spam in that it is designed to fool people into clicking on a malicious link or providing sensitive information.

It is often hard to tell when an email is a phishing mail or when it is real. Figure 1.1 shows a typical phishing email. The email is similar to what the reader expects from the impersonating organization, but if the reader looks closely, the language is enough off that it should raise concerns.

Proxies serve a number of different purposes, but currently their primary purpose is to mask the identity of the user requesting content and to protect users from visiting Web sites that are known to be bad sites. That was not always the case. Initially, proxies also served as caching proxies. To conserve network bandwidth and improve speed for end users a proxy would retrieve popular sites and store a cache of those sites. Rather than reaching out to the site every time a user requested an update, the proxy would simply serve the local copy of the site, while periodically updating its cache. In the early days of Internet connectivity a site could be a FTP (File Transfer Protocol), Gopher, or Web site; today the site is generally a Web site.

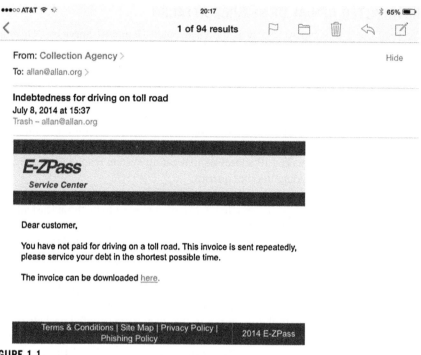

FIGURE 1.1

Screenshot of a typical phishing email.

This type of cached delivery is still common with large Web sites. These sites use Content Delivery Networks, such as Akamai, to bring content geographically and topologically closer to their clients.

The first Web proxy server was actually the CERN httpd server, which was developed for the NeXT platform and built in 1990. The NeXT platform was developed by Steve Jobs and his team at NeXT Computer Inc, after Jobs was ousted at Apple. Eventually NeXT was acquired by Apple and the NeXT operating system became the underpinning for both OS X and iOS at Apple. The CERN httpd server was primarily a Web server, but it had limited proxy functionality, including the ability to cache Web sites. Many consider the advent of the modern proxy to have arrived with the release of Squid in 1996. Squid is a development fork from the Harvest Cache Daemon codebase work done in the early 1990s. In addition to caching capabilities, squid also gave administrators the ability to block certain Web sites and even create limitations based on users and groups, functionality that exists in modern proxies.

Without using the term, proxy and spam filter administrators were amongst the first to use intelligence to secure their networks. Gathering the list of bad Web sites for proxies or known spam hosts for spam filters was an early form of cyber threat intelligence.

DISTRIBUTED DENIAL OF SERVICE ATTACKS

The final piece of security history is the Distributed Denial of Service (DDoS) attacks. Denial of Service (DoS) attacks have been around since the advent of the first piece of malware. It was very common for a virus to eat up system resources, sometimes unintentionally, sometime not, to the point that the machine became unusable and had to be rebooted or worse. But a DDoS attack is an attack against an entire network that originates from thousands or hundreds of thousands of hosts.

The first recorded DDoS attacks were in 1989 using simple ping flooding (Defense.net, 2014), which sends out large Internet Control Messaging Protocol (ICMP) packets usually from spoofed IP addresses that eat up system resources and prevent that system from responding to other queries.

Other notable DDoS tactics included smurf and fraggle attacks. A smurf attack occurred when an attacker sent a spoofed ICMP ping request to the broadcast address on a network. The request would be distributed to all of the hosts on the network and every host on that network would now send a response to the spoofed (victim) host. The name smurf comes from the tool smurf.c, which was released by TFreak in 1997. These attacks became so common that a new RFC had to be introduced. RFC 2644, released in 1999, mandates that routers not pass along broadcast packets. Because every network lies behind a router, smurf attacks became ineffective.

Fraggle attacks were similar in design in that they were spoofed packets sent to broadcast addresses. However, instead of being spoofed ICMP ping packets, they were spoofed packets to UDP (User Datagram Protocol) ports 7 and 19 (the chargen [Character Generator Protocol] port). Again, passing along broadcast packets is no longer allowed, and most organizations block all ports at the firewall, especially ports like UDP 7 and 19, which are no longer widely used.

As DDoS attacks grew in popularity so did the capability and sophistication of the tools used in these DDoS attack. In 1997 growth in sophistication resulted in the release of the DDoS-specific tool Trin00. Trin00 resided on compromised hosts and was controlled by a master. The Trin00 master would send commands to the daemons telling them to initiate the attacks. The daemons would then launch UDP-flooding attacks against a specified IP address.

The rise of DDoS attacks also led to the rise of botnets. For an attacker to be effective, it was necessary for the attacker to control thousands or even hundreds of thousands of compromised hosts. Of course, with control of those hosts an attacker was able to do more than just launch DDoS attacks. With a large botnet an attacker could launch spam and phishing campaigns, spread malware to other hosts on compromised networks and collect usernames, passwords, and other personal data.

UNIFIED THREAT MANAGEMENT

In 2012 Gartner reported for the first time that the Unified Threat Management (UTM) market was larger than $1 billion in size (Gartner Analysts, 2012). At a time when many security companies were struggling, the UTM market was experiencing double-digit growth, and it is easy to see why.

A UTM platform combines several different security functions such as firewall, VPN, mail filtering, proxy, and IDS into a single appliance with a single management console. The appeal of a UTM is obvious, overburdened security teams did not need to check three or four different consoles to track down a security incident. UTMs saved money, increased efficiency, sped up response times, and, usually, improved security within an organization.

Smaller companies were the early adopters of UTM technology. Large companies feared, not without foundation, that trying to support that much functionality with large amounts of traffic would cause slowdown.

As UTM technology continued to develop, companies like Cisco, Palo Alto, and Check Point delivered additional services on blades, which allowed them to support even larger organizations. Today, some of the largest organizations in the world rely, at least in part, on UTM technologies to secure their networks.

The rise of UTM technology adoption also rekindled the debate around single-vendor security solutions. A single-vendor security solution is when an organization relies on one vendor for all of their security needs. There are some advantages to this as it usually means that all of the solutions work together, which makes it easier for security teams to track a security incident through the network and speeds up remediation. There is also a commonality of security reporting within devices from the same vendor: A vulnerability rated critical in one platform will be rated critical in the same platform from that vendor. Similarly, the same nomenclature is used to describe threats across all devices from a single vendor, so if a bot is referred to as Zbot on one device it won't be called ZeuS on another.

On the other side of the argument, too much homogeny can cause security incidents to be missed. In single-vendor networks a threat may emerge that the adopted security vendor is slow to recognize, leaving organizations exposed for longer periods than those organizations with a mixed-vendor solution. Another potential issue is that even though a single-vendor solution should provide continuity between platforms, that is not always the case. Too many security companies have grown by acquisition. This acquisition strategy resulted in different technologies within the same security vendor being created and maintained by different teams who developed in silos and products within the same security vendor unable to communicate with each other. This situation is changing as more organizations are demanding interoperability from same-vendor solutions, but it is still a problem many organizations face.

UNDERSTANDING THE CURRENT THREAT

The threats outlined in the previous section still exist and have continued to evolve over the years. Network security has, unfortunately, not evolved nearly as fast as the threats have. In fact, in many organizations responsibility for network security has devolved and been divided into multiple groups who don't necessarily communicate with each other.

In a typical good-sized network there is usually a team dedicated to managing the desktop environment, that team manages the antivirus and collects desktop and server logs. Another team manages the mail server and spam filter, often the Web proxy as well. Finally, security team is usually responsible for the IDS and possibly the firewall (though that can be the responsibility of the network team).

This creates a situation in which security data are available in multiple consoles that are seen by different groups, with no correlation of data between consoles and usually between those groups. Each incident occurs inside a vacuum with no contextual information to determine the extent of the threat or whether any remediation steps that were undertaken were effective.

For example, if Alice is responsible for maintaining the antivirus system and she detects that a worm was flagged and quarantined on Bob's system, she might think a security incident has been averted, but if that worm was just one of two payload's that the initial loader put down, Bob may still be infected. When Carol sees that the firewall stopped a connection from Bob's machine to a host over port 6667 (IRC), she may think the problem is solved not realizing that Dave saw a connection to the same host over port 80 (HTTP) pass successfully through the proxy, also from Bob's machine.

Because attackers have become increasingly sophisticated, dividing up and isolating different security roles within an organization makes it more difficult to identify and successfully remediate attacks. Actually, that is not necessarily true. Some attackers are more sophisticated, most attackers benefit from the fact that the tools available to them are significantly more sophisticated and easier to use than ever before.

THE BUSINESS OF MALWARE

Cybercrime is a big business. According to some estimates, there is a $114 billion industry associated with cyber criminal activity. It is also a well-organized and hierarchical economy with many different moving parts. Someone who knows where to look and who has the right references could be launching attacks within a few hours.

According to a 2014 report by the RAND Corporation (Ablon et al, 2014) there are several roles within the cyber security underground market. Broadly speaking, RAND divides underground users into seven groups:

1. Administrators
2. Subject-matter experts
3. Intermediaries/brokers
4. Vendors
5. Witting mules
6. General members
7. Unwitting mules

The seven types of users of the market form a hierarchical structure with administrators and subject-matter experts sitting at the top of the hierarchy. These are the underground members who research and uncover zero-day vulnerabilities then figure out how to weaponize those vulnerabilities (e.g. turn them into usable exploits) or sell them. They also develop and continuously improve malware families, which are sold or rented to users who are lower in the hierarchy. Sometimes, but not always, these users are also actively engaged in attack activity.

In the middle tier of the RAND hierarchy exist the intermediaries/brokers and vendors. This is, in effect, the merchant tier. They are responsible for many of the transactions that occur on the underground. They will often sell malware on behalf of the upper tier members; they also help facilitate the sale of data collected from a successful breach.

This is one of the ways in which the cybercrime underground market mirrors traditional markets: distribution channels are important. If someone in the lower tiers gains access to a large network and is able to exfiltrate hundreds of thousands or, as is often the case, millions, of bits of personal data – whether that is credit card numbers, usernames and password, social security numbers – that person needs a way to sell the data. Someone in the lower tiers of the black market does not have access to and the trust of a large audience of buyers. In that the lower user will provide the data to a broker who will sell the data in return for percentage of the total sale.

The other way the underground market mirrors traditional markets is that it very much follows the law of supply in demand. In its 2014 Internet Security Threat Report (ISTR) (Symantec, 2014), Symantec referred to 2013 as the year of the "Mega Breach." During 2013 Symantec identified 253 breaches, eight of which exposed more than 10 million identities. Overall, in 2013 there were more than 550 identities exposed. Although this number is disturbing in its own right, it also has the effect of lowering the value of identity theft on the underground market. Where credit card information used to go for $5–$20 per record, depending on the information included with the sale (e.g. CVV, pin, etc), in 2013 credit card information was often valued at less than a dollar a record. In other words, there is so much attack activity occurring and it is occurring so regularly that the market has been flooded with personally identifiable information and lowered the value of that data to almost nothing.

COMMODITIZATION OF MALWARE

A large part of the growth data breeches can be directly attributed to the commoditization of malware. It used to be that if someone wanted to break into a network and maintain long-term access.

That is no longer the case. With tools like Metasploit, PhishPoll, and SpearPhisher it is easier than ever for an inexperienced attacker to launch a campaign at a specific target or flail around and accidentally stumble into multiple networks.

Of course, it is not enough to be able to gain access to the network; an attacker has to have something to leave behind in order to continue exploring the network and exfiltrate data out. Again, the underground market comes to the rescue with many malware families available for sale (see Figure 1.2).

FIGURE 1.2

Malware for sale on a Russian forum.

Developers who have had success in building malware are now, thanks to the underground market, able to sell their malware to other users. Pardon the corporate-speak, but this is really a win–win for both parties. For the developer, selling the malware is often more profitable than selling the data from breaches; for the buyer, the malware is a proven program that has had a lot of the bugs worked out. Just like traditional software sales, buying malware usually includes email and phone support during normal business hours and often a Service Level Agreement (SLA) for the life of the malware, which is until antivirus vendors identify it. Some malware for sale even comes with try-before-you-buy option that allows users to try out stripped down version and buy the full version if they like it.

Another example of the underground economy mimicking the traditional economy: In late 2010 there was a lot of discussion about two of the most popular malware kits ZeuS and SpyEye being set to merge. The original author of the ZeuS malware kit thought that authorities were getting too close, so he was going to hand over the code to the team behind SpyEye. There is some speculation as to whether or not that happened. Some ZeuSS source code did end up in the SpyEye kit, but not until after the ZeuS source code was leaked online, which had the added benefit of significantly driving down the cost of buying the ZeuS malware kit.

Of course, just as many businesses are moving software to the cloud so are malware users and developers. Rather than go through the trouble of learning how a piece of malware works and making sure it is properly updated many new and experienced attackers will simply rent the infrastructure they need for the time they need it.

Vendors in the underground market will build out the malware infrastructure, acquire the necessary redirecting structure, and ensure that the latest version of the malware is available and tested. Literally, all the would-be attacker needs to do is provide the list of emails the attacker desires to target and possibly an email template for the phishing lure.

If phishing is not the goal, there are other vendors who rent out their botnets for DDoS attacks or other nefarious purposes. Some attackers have amassed botnets with tens or hundreds of thousands systems that they control from a single console. For the right price they will activate that botnet and point it in the direction of any organization. These huge botnets are often able to diminish access to organizations for days or weeks at a time, either for revenge or to mask the real attack.

The barrier to entry is no longer having the technical skills and the time to develop and deploy the skills necessary to launch an attack against organizations. The barrier now is simply having enough money (and not very much is needed to get started) to rent or buy the tools from someone who is, essentially, a full-time malware developer.

To further highlight this underground market, in July 2014 iSIGHT Partners observed cyber criminals in underground networks offering, on Russian forums, to install malware on compromised hosts at an average price of $200 per 1000 hosts, and on Chinese forums at a price between $16 and $32 per 1000 hosts. In the same report iSIGHT also noted that Chinese forums were also offering DDoS capabilities for as low as $32 per hour (iSIGHT Partners, 2014).

THE KING PHISH

Any hacking movie or television show worth its salt will show viewers the intrepid hacker finding a hole in the firewall and breaking into the server to get the necessary data and pulling it back (usually with a bunch of irrelevant code flashing across the screen). As undoubtedly anyone reading this book knows, that is not the way the modern attack works. Most attacks start in gooey center. Why? Those attacks are the most effective.

Security teams have gotten very good at protecting the perimeter. Solid firewall rules and quickly updated IDS signatures keep attackers at bay. Although the occasional attacker has success with a SQL injection or an exposed port in the breaking into a network from the outside has become time-consuming and costly, with very little pay-off.

Phishing, on the other hand, is easy. It is so easy that in the 2014 ISTR Symantec (Symantec, 2014) reported that Symantec tracked 779 different phishing campaigns during 2013. These are campaigns that targeted a specific organization and were launched, according to the report, over an average of an 8-day period. Launching a few emails at a time within the organization allows the attacker to fly under the radar of the security systems in place and successfully infect more users.

Another reason why phishing, especially spear phishing, attacks are gaining in popularity is that it is easier than ever to track down a target's email address. Part of this is that the realm of phishing has moved from the personal to the professional. Yes, there are still the fake "Bank of America" emails out there, and there will be for the foreseeable future, but those are far less effective than they were. Phishing campaigns targeting an organization can be easy to set up and very effective, with the right lure.

How easy is it to get a list of email addresses within an organization? Depending on the size of the organization it can be a matter of minutes. There are, of course, lists of corporate users for sale in the underground. But if an attacker does not want to spend the money for a possibly outdated list of targets, the attacker has other options. Almost all organizations use the same pattern for their email addresses: *firstname_lastname@organization, firstinitiallastname@organization, lastname.firstname@organization*, and so on. All an attacker needs is one person's email address from within the organization and the attacker will know the email format. Next the attacker can head over to LinkedIn or Facebook and search for people who list that organization as their employer. Now, the attacker has a list of users along with their email addresses and can launch the spear phishing campaign.

Because the attacker knows the organization, it is surprisingly easy to craft an email that will entice users specifically within that organization to click the link or open an attachment. There are even Web sites (and videos for those too lazy to read) that offer advice on crafting successful lures while avoiding spam detection rules.

THE ATTACK SURFACE IS EXPANDING

According to the RAND paper (Ablon et al, 2014) mentioned earlier, credentials to an organization's Twitter account are worth more than credit card data. This makes sense; after all, posting a link to an infected site on a popular Twitter feed can result in significantly more infected users plus it has the added bonus of tarnishing that organization's brand in a very public way.

So, security teams that are struggling to keep up with the data they are collecting from firewalls, IDSs, proxies, and antivirus systems now need to worry about whether the marketing team is taking proper precautions on their social media accounts.

The bad news does not stop there. As fast as the growth in PC-based malware is, it is nothing compared to the growth in mobile malware. In 2013, Fortinet identified 1800 new families of malware (Fortinet, 2014), most of them targeting the ubiquitous Android platform. Although mobile malware is nothing new, with the rise of the smart phone, the capability, sophistication, and danger posed by mobile malware is a significant threat.

The mobile malware threat presents itself in a number of ways. Organizations that supply their employees with smart phones often are lenient when it comes to allowing users to install personal apps or check personal email on those phones. With those activities come increased risks, risks that often are not being monitored.

According to a report by RiskIQ in 2013 there were more than 11,000 apps that engaged in malicious behavior available at the Google Play Store (Miners, 2014). Although that number may be small compared to the total number of apps on the store, it still poses a significant threat.

That is not the only way that mobile malware can infect networks. In 2013 an app called Superclean, which advertised itself as an antivirus program for the Android platform, was the first piece of mobile malware identified that could jump from the phone to the PC. Now employees who brings their own phones to work and simply plug it into their office computers to charge it can infect the whole network.

There was also a rise in the number of watering hole attacks targeting specific organizations in 2013. A watering hole attack occurs when an attacker compromises a Web site that the attacker knows is frequented by organizations the attacker is targeting. For example, if the attacker is interested in gaining access to the financial industry, the attacker might compromise a financial news site frequented by those in the industry. Watering hole compromises tend to be against smaller, specialized sites that have a very specific audience. These sites don't usually have a strong security posture and can often be easier targets. The targets of the attack also trust the watering hole sites, so there little notice paid to any security anomalies that may occur when visiting the site.

Another way that the attack surface is expanding is through the rise of campaigns. A campaign is when a group of attackers decide to target a specific industry or event. The group Anonymous gained notoriety for their campaigns, usually advertised on Twitter with hashtags such as #OpUSA, #OpPetrol, and #OpWorldCup. But other groups use the same campaign strategy, pulling resources to target the financial industry, defense industrial base, and other high-profile targets. Oftentimes, smaller organizations can be collateral damage in these campaigns or they can be targeted so they can be used to gain access to the larger organizations in that industry. Another trend in attack activity is that attackers are targeting smaller and smaller organizations.

Even as recently as 2010, attackers launching targeted attacks went after large or high-profile organizations almost exclusively. These organizations quickly learned to beef up their network security and became much more difficult to target. Because of that, attackers learned that they could go after smaller, less-secure organizations and used those compromised organizations to not only gather vast quantities of data, but also as a springboard to the get to the larger organizations. In fact in the 2014 ISTR (Symantec, 2014), Symantec noted that although 39% of all targeted attacks were aimed at large enterprises (defined as 2501 or more employees), a full 30% of targeted attacks were aimed at small businesses (defined as 250 or fewer employees).

It is no longer enough for the security team to monitor what is happening in their network; it is just as important to be aware of the threat that is surrounding their organization. It is important to know what is happening outside of their network and how that impacts other organizations in their vertical.

The rise of the cloud

It started simply; network teams weren't comfortable managing hosting and email services so they outsourced to third-party hosting companies. But the number of services delivered to employees through the cloud has grown dramatically over the years. Companies like ADP, Workday, SalesForce.com, DocuSign, DropBox, and many others are moving critical organization functions to the cloud. The benefits of a cloud-centered organization vary from making it easier for remote employees to access critical services to expanding the offerings available to employees in general.

The downside to cloud services is that they become part of the expanding attack surface and security teams generally have little insight into the security posture of those services. Of course, it is not just the security team; most organizations do not have any insight into the security of their data hosted in the cloud.

That is not to say that cloud providers do not take security seriously. Most have excellent security controls in place and take the protection of their customer data very seriously. But most cloud providers do not make security logs and indicators available to their customers, which means there may be attacks, even thwarted attacks, occurring against customer data that the customer does not know about. Even when these providers do make logs available, those logs are often only available in the cloud, with no easy way to pull them into the organization's network, meaning the security team now has multiple consoles for its cloud providers that need to be reviewed regularly, on top of all their other work.

This creates a problem for security teams trying to correlate data across expanding attack vectors. For example, an attacker may attempt to access an employee's DropBox folder to gain access to valuable documents, and may also try to launch a spear phishing attack against that employee. The security team may know about the second attack, but not the first, meaning there is no correlation of activity between the two events. This would lead the security team to the erroneous conclusion that it was a one-time attack, successfully foiled, rather than a persistent attack in which the attacker is likely looking for a new attack vector.

This is in no way a condemnation of cloud services. Cloud providers deliver a valuable, and increasingly critical, service to their clients but they also can make the job of securing the network even more difficult than it already is.

THE COMING THREATS

A recap of the discussion so far: The network is not safe, the systems on the network are not safe, cell phones are not safe, email is not safe, Web sites are not safe, social media is not safe, and other organizations are not safe. It seems like every surface that an attacker could use to launch attacks is covered. What else is left?

To start with, it is going to get worse. To many, already overwhelmed, security teams the thought that it could get worse seems inconceivable. But the fact is that just two things keep cyber attacks at bay today: knowledge and infrastructure.

There are a lot of hotspots of knowledge around the world, but not as many as there are hotspots of activity. Consider, for example, Iran. Iran currently engages in a lot of attack activity, but the attacks tend to be less sophisticated than what is seen coming out of Russia or China. Yet, pockets of Iranian attacks have shown increasing sophistication and that sophistication will trickle down to other groups within Iran.

Conversely, there are a number of countries that have a sophisticated technical populace but limited infrastructure. Pakistan is a good example. Pakistan has a great number of schools that focus on technology studies, but it has poor infrastructure. This makes launching large-scale attacks impossible. As Pakistan improves its infrastructure, expect to see more attacks originating from the region.

So, in the future there will be more attacks, originating from more regions of the world and the attacks will become more sophisticated. The term *advanced persistent threat* (APT) is thrown around too frequently in marketing literature and sales meetings. APT is vaguely used to describe a sophisticated, targeted attack – often associated with nation–state activity. The problem with the term is that most targeted attacks are indistinguishable from what most would consider an APT in terms of sophistication, tradecraft, and persistence. The mega breaches that occurred in 2013 and that were described earlier in this chapter were, for the most part, sophisticated and targeted, and went on for months.

Those attacks, which were not referred to APT attacks in the press, have all the elements of an APT attack, minus the nation–state backing. The tools available to even the most basic attacker rival those of the tools that are available to many nation–states.

Not only are attacks going to occur more frequently, become more sophisticated and originate from more places, but they will also become more destructive.

When it was first uncovered in 2010, the Stuxnet worm made headlines because of its sophistication. The virus targeted very specific components within power plants and appears to have been designed specifically to alter components common in Iranian power plants. Since the discovery of Stuxnet there have been at least other destructive worms uncovered by researchers: Duqu, Flame, and Shamoon. Each was designed to target a specific Supervisory Control and Data Acquisition (SCADA) system and potentially damage that system.

As attackers become more aggressive and tools become more sophisticated, expect to see more worms that include destructive capabilities.

Stuxnet, and malware like Stuxnet, highlight another aspect of future malware: specialization. Today's malware is, for the most part, one size fits all. Once a server is compromised, the malware is installed and modules are uploaded for different functionality. For example, if the attacker needs a key logger installed on the system he simply uploads the key logger module to the compromised host and everything continues to communicate through the same installed malware.

That model works great for basic tasks, but it does not work well for specialized needs. To that end malware developers are designing purpose-built malware to complete specific tasks.

A prime example of that is the rash of Point of Sale (POS) compromises in 2013 and 2014. These compromises used POS-specific malware like BlackPOS and Dexter, which are designed to look for credit card numbers and their accompanying information in the memory of the systems on which they are installed. They look for specifically formatted data, intercept that data, and send command and control host where it is stored until it can be sold on the underground market. As with other forms of malware, POS malware is available for sale or rent on the underground market.

Moving forward expect to see more purpose-built malware with specific tasks or targeting specific data types. Also expect these purpose-built programs to work closely with the more popular malware programs out there. The better these programs interoperate with each other, the easier it will be for new users to operate them and the more money those in the background developing the programs will make.

CONCLUSION

Up to this point, threat intelligence has not been a major part of the discussion. But intelligence is what is going to move security forward and allow security teams with limited time and budget to succeed against the onslaught of threats, both present and future threats.

Of course, threat intelligence is not enough. There are dozens, if not hundreds, of organizations that are touting threat intelligence. In some cases, threat intelligence can make the problem of securing the network worse. Improperly ingested threat intelligence can overwhelm an already struggling security team and produce more false-positives than true security events.

That is why bringing intelligence into a security organization is not enough. To successfully protect the network, the security team must learn how to transform from a reactionary, event-driven team to a proactive intelligence-driven one.

It is not an easy task. With the amount of malware and the number of attacks continuing to grow and the attack surface expanding trying to get a handle on everything within the network as well as understanding the threats outside the network is a daunting task. Compounding the problem is most organizations are reducing security budgets, and often department sizes.

The rest of this section of the book delves into the concept of intelligence and how organizations can build an intelligence model that can be used to effectively and continuously protect their network.

REFERENCES

Ablon, L., Libicki, M.C., Golay, A.A., 2014. Markets for cybercrime tools and stolen data: hacker's bazaar. <http://www.rand.org/content/dam/rand/pubs/research_reports/RR600/RR610/RAND_RR610.pdf>. (accessed 11.07.14.).

Cohen, F., 1984. A computer virus. <http://www.all.net/books/virus/>. (accessed 10.07.14.).

Defense.net, 2014. DDoS attack timeline. <http://www.defense.net/ddos-attack-timeline.html>. (accessed 11.07.14.).

Defense Advanced Research Projects Agency (DARPA), 1981. Transmission control protocol: DARPA internet program protocol specification. <https://www.ietf.org/rfc/rfc793.txt>. (accessed 14.10.14.).

DNEWS Editors, 2011. First computer virus, creeper, was no bug. <http://news.discovery.com/tech/first-computer-virus-creeper-was-no-bug-110316.htm>. (accessed 10.07.14.).

Denning, D.E., 1987. An intrusion detection model. IEEE Trans Softw Eng. 13 (2), 222–232.

Fortinet, 2014. 2014 Threat landscape report. <http://www.fortinet.com/sites/default/files/whitepapers/Threat-Landscape-2014.pdf>. (accessed 11.07.14.).

Gartner Analysts, 2012. Gartner says worldwide unified threat management market surpassed the $1 billion mark in 2011. <http://www.gartner.com/newsroom/id/1991815>. (Accessed July 11th 2014)(accessed 11.07.14.).

Gudkova, D., 2014. Kaspersky Security Bulletin. Spam evolution 2013. <http://securelist.com/analysis/kaspersky-security-bulletin/58274/kaspersky-security-bulletin-spam-evolution-2013/>. (accessed 11.07.14.).

iSIGHT Partners, 2014. Overview of cybercrime services available for sale online.

Kaspersky Labs, 2013. Number of the year: Kaspersky Lab is detecting 315,000 new malicious files every day. <http://www.kaspersky.com/about/news/virus/2013/number-of-the-year>. (accessed 10.07.14.).

Leydon , J., 2012. The 30-year-old prank that became the first computer virus. <http://www.theregister.co.uk/2012/12/14/first_virus_elk_cloner_creator_interviewed/>. (accessed 10.07.14.).

Miners, Z., 2014. Report: malware-infected Android apps spike in the Google Play store. <http://www.pcworld.com/article/2099421/report-malwareinfected-android-apps-spike-in-the-google-play-store.html>. (accessed 12.07.14.).

Phishing.org, (n.d.). History of phishing. <http://www.phishing.org/history-of-phishing/>. (accessed 11.07.14.).

Seltzer, Larry, 2013. ZDNet: the Morris Worm: Internet malware turns 25 <http://www.zdnet.com/the-morris-worm-internet-malware-turns-25-7000022740/>. (accessed 03.07.14.).

Symantec, 2014. Internet Security Threat Report 2014. <http://www.symantec.com/content/en/us/enterprise/other_resources/b-istr_main_report_v19_21291018.en-us.pdf>. (accessed 11.07.14.).

Zakon, R., 2014. Hobbes' Internet timeline 11. <http://www.zakon.org/robert/internet/timeline/>. (accessed 03.07.14.).

What is intelligence?

## 2

INFORMATION IN THIS CHAPTER:

- Defining Intelligence
- The Intelligence Cycle
- Types of Intelligence
- The Professional Analyst
- Denial and Deception
- Intelligence Throughout the Ages

INTRODUCTION

Intelligence is just starting to come into its own within the realm of cyber security, but intelligence as a discipline has a long history in the world of the military and government. In fact, intelligence has existed since before it was a formalized discipline. As discussed later in this chapter, leaders like Sun Tzu and Julius Caesar had very rigorous and well-documented intelligence processes that they followed. These processes contributed greatly to their success – and allowed other leaders to learn from them.

Likewise, today there are many security teams that, knowingly or unknowingly, engage in many of the best intelligence practices. But most of the time, intelligence practices are haphazardly implemented without an eye to the big picture.

The goal of this chapter is to help the reader understand some of the best intelligence practices outside of the realm of network security. By first understanding the fundamentals of intelligence, as a discipline, organizations can take the best practices and use those practices to improve the effectiveness of the network security teams.

A single chapter is not enough to cover all aspects of the intelligence discipline, or to dive deeply into any one topic. Instead, the hope is to start a discussion about changing the way network security is thought of within an organization and improve the ability of teams to effectively address the most important challenges facing their organization.

DEFINING INTELLIGENCE

Despite the fact that the military and governments have engaged in intelligence activities for thousands of years, there is surprisingly little consensus about the definition of intelligence. A quick review of literature shows a range of definitions, none of which seems complete.

The CIA defines intelligence as (CIA, 1999):

Reduced to its simplest terms, intelligence is knowledge and foreknowledge of the world around us — the prelude to decision and action by US policymakers.

On the other hand, the FBI uses the following definition (FBI, 2014):

Simply defined, intelligence is information that has been analyzed and refined so that it is useful to policymakers in making decisions – specifically, decisions about potential threats to our national security.

The Department of Defense (DOD) defines intelligence as (DOD, 2014):

The product resulting from the collection, processing, integration, evaluation, analysis, and interpretation of available information concerning foreign nations, hostile or potentially hostile forces or elements, or areas of actual or potential operations.

The FBI and DOD definitions of intelligence view intelligence as either a product or a process, and there is no doubt those are important parts of the definition, but they are also limiting. The CIA definition is broad, may be even too broad, but it takes into account that intelligence involves understanding the context of the data collected.

The definition of intelligence has been debated in scholarly journals for years. One problem in creating a more focused definition is that different groups have different uses for intelligence. A military commander in the field has different needs than a legislative body attempting to write policy based on intelligence.

No matter the role of the end user for intelligence, intelligence, at its core, is information. However, not all information is intelligence. As Michael Warner (2007) writes in *Wanted: A Definition of "Intelligence": Understanding Our Craft*, "For producers of intelligence, however, the equation 'intelligence = information' is too vague to provide real guidance in their work." After his review of the literature, Warner (2007) comes up with the following definition:

Intelligence is secret, state activity to understand or influence foreign entities.

This gets pretty close to a workable definition, but it ignores the fact that not all intelligence is secret. Especially in the age of Google, open source intelligence (OSINT) has become a critical tool in the arsenal of the intelligence analyst.

Gill and Phythian (2012) noticed the same deficiency in Warner's definition and they expanded on it in their book *Intelligence in an Insecure World* with the following:

Intelligence is the umbrella term referring to the range of activities – from planning and information collection to the analysis and dissemination – conducted in secret and aimed at maintaining or enhancing relative security by providing forewarning of threats or potential threats in a manner that allows for the timely implementation of a preventive policy or strategy, including, where deemed desirable, covert activities.

Although this definition is longer than Warner's, it is more complete and it makes an important distinction: what data being collected should be kept secret from the enemy, but the data itself does not necessarily have to be secret.

Even though Gill and Phythian's proposed definition is among the most complete, there is still a nagging problem with all modern definitions of intelligence: the focus is only on the external. Stepping back from modern definitions for a second, Sun Tzu (2012a), who is often quoted by network security professionals, wrote the following in *The Art of War*:

Hence the saying: If you know the enemy and know yourself, you need not fear the result of a hundred battles.

A well-run organization cannot have an effective intelligence program without a complete and honest assessment of its own strengths and weaknesses. Not only is that assessment critical, it should be performed on a regular basis – this allows leaders to make informed decisions as to the best preventive policy or strategy.

Without attempting to rewrite the definition of intelligence, keep in mind that knowing what is happening within an organization or even country can be just as important as what is happening outside.

THE INTELLIGENCE CYCLE

To create a successful intelligence program, an organization needs a framework within which it can operate. A framework helps to establish the ways in which intelligence will be gathered and delivered. It should be open enough to operate in multiple environments and timeframes, and be usable by different groups in the organization. At the same time it should be restrictive enough that it helps push a professional environment with clearly defined roles.

Most organizations use a variation of the intelligence cycle outlined in Figure 2.1 as their framework for building and maintaining an intelligence organization.

The intelligence cycle in Figure 2.1 works because it has clearly defined roles built around a specific mission. The model is also portable enough to be used for both large-scale and small-scale missions, often simultaneously. On the one hand, the mission could be "Protect the United States"; it could also be "Determine al-Shabaab's Weapons Capabilities." Note, that the two missions are not necessarily mutually exclusive: learning more about the weapons capabilities of the terrorist group al-Shabaab could increase the security of the United States. One intelligence cycle can inform other cycles.

FIGURE 2.1

The intelligence cycle.

Another important aspect of the intelligence cycle is that is intentionally designed as a circle, because the cycle is continuous. Once the mission has been assigned planning and direction are handled by the organization's leaders. Data is collected, processed and delivered to an analysis team for review who publish the data to the required parties. The results of the intelligence analysis drives new intelligence requirements which leads the leadership to task the collection team to begin gathering data, and the process continues.

In addition to being a continuous loop, there should also be feedback from different groups within the organization throughout the process. A well-run intelligence organization does not rely on leadership to facilitate communication between the various teams. For intelligence teams to operate effectively, there has to be open communication and information sharing between the teams – teams that are working on the same mission as well as teams that have a different mission.

The intelligence cycle starts, ends, and starts again with planning and direction. The planning and direction team are the managers of the entire intelligence cycle. This phase involves receiving requirements from policy makers or military officials, or building new requirements based on the feedback from previously released intelligence. The team uses the mission and the direction from the consumers of the intelligence to produce intelligence requirements that get passed on the collection team.

The collections team is responsible for carrying out the requirements passed on from the planning and direction. Members of this team are responsible for devising systems that meet the collection needs of the planning and direction teams. There are six different areas of intelligence collection:

- SIGINT: Signals intelligence – data collected, usually surreptitiously, from electronic systems.

- OSINT: Open source intelligence – publicly available data from news sources, radio, or the Internet.
- HUMINT: Human-sourced intelligence – intelligence collected from human sources, wittingly or unwittingly.
- IMINT: Imagery intelligence – data collected via images, whether those images are photographs, a radar screen or some other method of representation.
- GEOINT: Geospatial intelligence – intelligence gathered from satellite, drones, and other sources that track security-related activity around the planet and derive intelligence from those movements. Often closely associated with IMINT.
- MASINT: Measurement and signature intelligence – almost a catchall, MASINT intelligence is derived from sources that do not fall into SIGINT or IMINT, such as radio frequencies.

At this point in the intelligence cycle, no intelligence has been created. Rather, the collections team is responsible for collecting information, with little or no filter applied to the gathered data. The sole responsibility of the collection team is to fulfill the intelligence requirements by gathering as much data as possible and throwing that data to the processing and exploitation team.

The processing and exploitation team is responsible for the first filtering of the data collected by the collections team. This may require translating information, transcribing data, decrypting data, or converting the data into a format that the analysts are able to read. The processing and exploitation team acts as a conduit between collections and analysis, as well as being the first attempt at filtering the amount of data received.

The analysis and production team is responsible for sifting through the raw data gathered by the collections team and building a narrative around an event, activity or group. It is a very challenging job because it often requires piecing together fragments of disparate data collected from a range of sources and determining what is really happening. Analysts are experts in their field and have the ability to take complex situations and information and distill it to the point where a lay audience is able to understand the nuances of an event, group, or action.

The next stage is dissemination. Once intelligence has been produced and gone through the vetting process it is considered finished intelligence (FINTEL for short). FINTEL cannot sit in a vacuum; it must be distributed to the original consumers as well as to other groups that have a need to know the information contained within the FINTEL.

By definition, the intelligence cycle does not end with dissemination of information. Upon receiving FINTEL consumers of that intelligence should have additional questions or requests for refinement of the results. It is these requests that drive additional intelligence requirements that generate new collection requests and push the intelligence cycle. Well-written and well-sourced intelligence often reaches new audiences, which drives new requests, and, ultimately, can improve the scope and capability of the collections team.

As FINTEL from an organization reaches a broader audience the planning team may find themselves receiving requests from consumers who are not well versed in the capabilities of the intelligence team. This often means guiding the requests from these users and helping them form actionable tasks.

Although it is important to remember that the customer is always right, sometimes it is the job of the planning and direction team to push the customer toward "rightness." An example of this is the often-told story of a professor who was working with graduate students to review survey data gathered from the incoming freshman class. As part of the survey the students had to include their student ID number. The professor asked the graduate students to include the mean, median, and mode of the student ID numbers. The graduate students explained that there was no value in the number, but the professor insisted the results be run and included in their report. The point is that not every request is going to make sense. It is important for the planning and direction team to not only understand which requests don't make sense, but to be able to explain why those requests don't make sense so as to prevent wasting the time of already overburdened collection and analyst teams.

There are three types of collection requirements: Critical Information Requirements (CIRs), Priority Information Requirements (PIRs), and Requests for Information (RFIs). CIRs are long-term collection requirements that help define the mission. A CIR can last for years and helps to define and refine the intelligence mission. It also guides the creation of other types of intelligence requests.

The second type of requirement, PIRs, are shorter-term requests that fall within the realm of existing CIRs. They are more narrowly focused, usually around a single aspect of a CIR. They help to paint a complete picture without changing the scope of the CIR.

The last type of requirement is the RFI. RFIs are short-term requests that produce quick answers, sometimes not even in the form FINTEL. They are very narrow in scope, but still must fall in-line with existing CIRs.

TYPES OF INTELLIGENCE

There are three different types of intelligence that an intelligence organization can produce: strategic, operational, and tactical. FINTEL can address all three types of intelligence in a single report, or it may only address a subset of these types, depending on the requirements and available data.

Each intelligence type serves a different purpose and targets a different audience. When traversing the intelligence cycle it is important to understand who the target audience is for a piece of FINTEL and the report must be geared to the audience. In other words, the intelligence needs to be actionable by the target group.

As Figure 2.2 outlines, the different types are hierarchical in nature with strategic intelligence at the top. Strategic intelligence is concerned with long-term trends surrounding threats, or potential threats to an organization. Strategic intelligence is forward thinking and relies heavily on estimation – anticipating future behavior based on past actions or expected capabilities. Effective strategic intelligence requires

FIGURE 2.2

The intelligence pyramid.

analysts with deep subject-matter expertise, as well as willingness to understand and adapt to changes in the adversary environment.

Tactical intelligence is an assessment of the immediate capabilities of an adversary. It focuses on the weaknesses, strengths, and the intentions of an enemy. An honest tactical assessment of an adversary allows those in the field to allocate resources in the most effective manner and engage the adversary at the appropriate time and with the right battle plan.

Operational intelligence is real time, or near real-time intelligence, often derived from technical means, and delivered to ground troops engaged in activity against the adversary. Operational intelligence is immediate, and has a short time to live (TTL). The immediacy of operational intelligence requires that analysts have instant access to the collection systems and be able to put together FINTEL in a high-pressure environment.[1]

As with the intelligence cycle, the three types of intelligence feed off each other and each has impact on the other types of intelligence. Strategic intelligence drives the requirements for tactical intelligence, which drives the requirements for operational intelligence. A successful operation may change the tactical intelligence picture, and a number of successful operations may change the strategic outlook.

THE PROFESSIONAL ANALYST

The importance of the analyst role has been touched on a number of times in this chapter. In an intelligence organization, the analyst is the one who ultimately decides what is and isn't important to be published as FINTEL. Intelligence failures throughout history have led to many disasters, from losing battles to being taken by complete surprise by major world events. No analyst is perfect, but there are ways that analysts can improve the way they think so as to make more effective decisions with less bias.

---

[1]For additional reading on the different types of intelligence check out George, R.Z., Bruce, J.B. (Eds.), 2008. Analyzing Intelligence: Origins, Obstacles, and Innovations. Georgetown University Press, Washington, DC.

A rigorous and disciplined thinking methodology, also known as tradecraft, is a critical linchpin in the intelligence process. But good analysis does not exist in a vacuum. If poor direction drives poor collection systems, leaving analysts with inaccurate or incomplete data, then the analysts will fail. Similarly, if analysts produce FINTEL that is ignored or even squelched by leadership, then it does not serve any purpose. If the leadership within an organization influences the results of the analysis process, it can cause irreparable damage to the reputation of the analysis team or organization, which is worse than ignoring intelligence.

The previous examples all sit outside of the analyst organization and are often outside of the direct control of the analyst team. There are, however, problems directly associated with analyst work, these problems revolve around cognitive bias. A cognitive bias is an error in the processing of information that leads to an incorrect conclusion, a distortion of information or an illogical determination. All humans suffer from cognitive bias; it would be impossible to get through life without some preconceived notion about how events are going to play out, an ability to anticipate the future. The problem is when those preconceived notions remain intact, even when the facts surrounding an event change. Cognitive bias has resulted in disaster for many nations over thousands of years.

In 1977, the CIA famously reported, "…the shah will be an active participant in Iranian life well into the 1980s." A year later the CIA would also report, "Iran is not in a revolutionary or even a 'prerevolutionary' state." Of course, on January 16, 1979 the Shah of Iran was forced to leave the country and Iran was taken over by religious clerics led by Ayatollah Ruhollah Khomeni (Walton, 2010a).

In fairness to the CIA, no other intelligence agency within the United States picked up on the potential for revolution, despite the fact that protests had been present and growing more vocal for two years prior to the overthrow. This example highlights one of the most dangerous cognitive biases that analysts can succumb to: the paradox of expertise.

The paradox of expertise often impacts the most experienced analysts. Analysts who are experts in a particular field and have spent many years studying a country, group, or individual will often miss or dismiss situational changes because those changes do not fit with the established pattern.

In the case of the Iranian Revolution, the analysts who were monitoring Iran were experts with long successful track records covering activity in Iran, but they were primarily relying on the Shah and his agents in the government and the military for their intelligence. The analysts had little association with the religious leaders or with the population of Iran in general. Because of that limited association, there were very few reports that contradicted what the analysts learned from their sources. What little contradictory reports there were went largely ignored.

Confirmation bias occurs when analysts pay more attention to those indicators that reinforce their beliefs, while discounting those indicators that contradict their beliefs. Confirmation bias is really about the weight assigned to indicators, based solely on whether or not those indicators agree with preconceived notions. For example, if a person is convinced that teenagers today are worse (given some definition of worse) than they were 30 years ago, that person might focus attention on news stories about crimes committed by teenagers and ignore news stories about the overall decline in teen criminal activity. Confirmation bias is especially prevalent in political discussions. Information from entire news outlets can be ignored simply because they are perceived to be too liberal or too conservative.

As with all cognitive biases, confirmation bias is not inherently a bad thing. The ability to judge the reputation of a source and to form a narrative around an event is important. In fact, for analysts this is a critical skill. The danger comes in when an analyst or a group of analysts refuse give serious consideration to competing hypothesis because those hypothesis don't fit with the current narrative, rather than accepting that the narrative may be changing (Davis, 2008).

One way to combat confirmation bias is to engage in "devil's advocacy." Devil's advocacy, in its simplest form, is the presentation of alternative hypotheses that offer a different, but plausible, explanation for current events. By forcing someone in the organization to adopt and defend multiple explanations, an organization can more fully explore alternative hypotheses and see if they don't, perhaps, offer a better explanation. For devil's advocacy to work, the competing narratives must all make sense and they must be rigorously defended. This type of engagement can help to adjust the narrative, sometimes in small ways, but may uncover a completely new narrative.

Another common cognitive bias that analysts succumb to is coherence bias. Coherence bias, sometimes referred to as mirror imaging, is the assumption that the groups or people being analyzed have the same motivations as the analysts. Coherence bias causes the analyst to assign the analyst's values to the subject of the analysis, which can cause the analyst to overlook vital information. In the example above, prior to the overthrow of the Shah there were reports that the clerics in Iran were amassing increasing amounts of power and with that power demanding the closure of liquor stores and other activities that they did not approve of for religious reasons. Because the analysts were used to living in a secular society, it was hard to imagine that religious leaders could amass as large a following as was being reported. In hindsight, it was clear the clerics were not only able to attract a large number of followers, but the followers had no qualms about living in a country that was, and still is, ruled by religious leaders.

Speaking of hindsight, hindsight bias is another common cognitive bias that plagues analysts. Of course, it does not just impact analysts; undoubtedly some people reading this section are wondering how the analysts could have been so wrong about the situation in Iran when the coming revolution was obvious.

Hindsight bias is more than simply saying, "How could anyone miss this event?" It often involves memory distortion, a phenomenon wherein memories are actually altered to fit the new narrative, most often expressed with the phrase, "I knew it all along." Hindsight bias can be dangerous because it makes it hard to provide rigorous methodological analysis to past events in order to learn from those events. No analyst is perfect; when mistakes are made it is important to be able to honestly analyze those mistakes and learn from them for future analysis.

Anchoring bias is another challenge facing analysts. Anchoring bias occurs when the analyst relies too heavily on one aspect of the collected data. In anchoring bias, a single piece of data is weighed more heavily than others. Often it is the first piece of intelligence gathered, but it does not need to be. Anchoring bias is a trap that many young analysts are especially susceptible to, but it doesn't only affect young analysts. Anchoring bias also affects people in the making of everyday decisions. Car dealerships, for example, rely heavily on customers focusing on the monthly payments versus the overall cost of the car or other features.

In the case of the Iranian Revolution, analysts at the CIA were anchored in their belief that the Shah could handle any troubles that arose. All intelligence gathered indicating the rise of the clerics and continued unrest of the population were viewed through the prism of a strong Shah able to easily handle the minor threats. Again, that turned out not be true, but because analysts accepted it as fact that is how they proceeded when producing FINTEL on the situation in Iran.

DENIAL AND DECEPTION

As if the job of an intelligence organization is not hard enough, it also has to contend with denial and deception from adversaries. An intelligence organization rarely has a complete picture of the adversary or target. Because of the diminished view, these intelligence organizations rely heavily on indicators – things like troop movements, intercepted communications, and inside information – to produce a complete picture of intelligence.

As mentioned before, intelligence collection does not exist in a vacuum. Adversaries are aware that they are being targeted and will take steps to prevent collection mechanisms or fool those mechanisms.

Denial, as a mechanism, seeks to prevent, or at least degrade, the ability to collect information by adversaries. It generally requires an understanding of the adversaries' capabilities as well as the ability to subvert those capabilities. Knowing what an adversary is capable of is not effective unless the target can also countermand those capabilities.

Deception involves manipulation collection systems either directly or indirectly. Deception can involve deliberately planting false information within collection systems, but it can also involve planting true but skewed information. The goal of deception is twofold: to spoil the collection systems with tainted information and to sway the thinking the analysts producing the FINTEL, causing the analysts to engage in one of the many forms of cognitive bias through the release of skewed information (Bruce and Bennett, 2008).

Planting false information does not just have to occur within collection systems, baiting is another form of deception that involves using lures to attract users in the target organization. For example, an attacker might place thumb drives with the logo of a tobacco company in an area where smokers from the target organization frequently gather. The employees pick up the thumb drives, take them into the office and plug them into their corporate desktops, not knowing that there is malware loaded on the thumb drive that will self-install upon insertion.

Diluting is another form of deception in a cyber security environment. Dilution is the idea of overwhelming a security team with so many alerts that they do not notice the real attack. This is most often used in the realm of Distributed Denial of Service (DDoS) attacks. A clever attacker will launch a series of DDoS attacks against a target organization, and while the security team is scrambling to deal with the DDoS attacks, the attacker will launch the real attack. A really clever attacker will not even launch the DDoS attack directly; instead the attacker will wait until someone else is launching an attack against the organization the attacker is targeting, or sometimes instigate a group to launch a targeted attack.

Denial and deception (D&D) are powerful tools in the hands of a target and can lead to costly intelligence failures. D&D campaigns are also problematic because, if they are done correctly, they are difficult to detect. Almost all of the time analysts only have a limited view of activity within a target. Taking that limited view and distorting it or denying access to important facts can go unnoticed. To that end, analysts must be cognizant of what they do not know and provide an accurate accounting of the gaps in their knowledge.

One of the largest and most successful D&D campaigns in history was Operation Fortitude, the campaign launched by the Allies to hide the D-Day assault against Germany that helped bring an end to World War II. It is hard to overstate the impressiveness of Operation Fortitude. The idea that the Allies were able to disguise the 156,000-troop assault on five beachheads at Normandy the morning of June 6, 1944 from the Germans until it was too late is a topic that is still written about.[2]

Operation Fortitude was divided into two parts: Fortitude North and Fortitude South. In its simplest form, the goal of Fortitude North was to convince the Germans that the Allies were attacking Norway, while the goal of Fortitude South was to convince Germany that the Allies were going to launch an attack against Pas-de-Calais, France.

How these operations were carried out was anything but simple. To succeed the Allies deployed a number of deceptions, including the use of double agents and fake troop deployments, which included dummy inflatable troops, sending radio transmissions with false information, and increasing radio activity in the targeted deception regions. All of this was coupled with the fact that the Bletchley Park team in London had access to a working replica of the German Enigma cipher machine. Consequently, the Allies were able to monitor the effectiveness of their deception campaign and adjust accordingly, something very rare in intelligence circles. In addition to the incredible work of the Allies, Operation Fortitude benefitted from the "incompetence" (Erskine and Smith, 2011) of the Abwehr, the German Intelligence Service. Because of infighting with other intelligence groups and a lack of resources, the Abwehr was particularly susceptible to D&D style campaigns.

---

[2]For a more detailed account, see Levine, J., 2011. Operation Fortitude: The Story of the Spies and the Spy Operation that Save D-Day. Lyons Press, Guilford, CT.

Today, the use of mathematics in encryption is a given, that was not the case in the 1930s. Although the team at Bletchley Park deserves all the praise that can be delivered to them for the amazing work they did during World War II, it was actually the Polish and French that cracked the Enigma cipher.

In 1932, Poland, concerned about Germany's rise to power, recruited a team of mathematicians to attempt to break the Enigma cipher. They were given a commercial copy of the Enigma machine and tried to reverse engineer the cipher. They were able to do so, but did not know how the wiring was different from the wiring in the Enigma machines designed for the German army.

That's where France came in. The French were able to acquire the operating instructions for the German army version of the Enigma as well as two sheets of monthly key settings. Combining the French intelligence with the brilliant work of the Polish mathematicians, the Polish intelligence service was able to break the code.

D&D are critical tools in the arsenal of organization that are being targeted. It is important for organizations to understand how to use D&D effectively, while at the same time have the resources in place to understand when they are being targeted by a D&D campaign.

INTELLIGENCE THROUGHOUT THE AGES

Intelligence as an independent discipline is a relatively new phenomenon, but intelligence has existed since there was conflict between tribes of early humans. Without knowing it, some of the most famous early leaders have lain out principles of intelligence that are still in use today. Before moving into the realm of cyber threat intelligence, it is important to take a look at some of the lessons from history.

SUN TZU

No single person has had a bigger impact on the intelligence discipline as Sun Tzu. It is rare to find an intelligence professional who does not have a copy of the *Art of War* and many can quote directly from it. There is a lot of disagreement surrounding the life of Sun Tzu, but most scholars believe he lived in the fifth century BCE and served as a general to the king of the Wu kingdom. *The Art of War* is believed to be a compendium of his thoughts on war based on his successes as a general. However, there is some debate as to whether or not *The Art of War* is solely the work of Sun Tzu, or a compilation of work from many different authors.

Irrespective of the origins of *The Art of War*, in the book Sun Tzu lays out many strategy and intelligence ideas still followed today. According to Sun Tzu (2012b) there are five aspects to a military campaign:

The art of war, then, is governed by the five constant factors, to be taken into account in one's deliberations, when seeking to determine the conditions obtaining in the field.
These are: (1) The Moral Law; (2) Heaven; (3) Earth; (4) The Commander; (5) Method and discipline.

When Sun Tzu referred to Moral Law he was talking about politics, ensuring that the kingdom was unified in the activity. Sun Tzu knew that even in a province ruled by a king that without public opinion a war had little chance of success. The people of the kingdom must have confidence in the leaders to wage war effectively, therefore be willing to deal with the dangers and sacrifice that war entails.

Heaven and Earth refer to weather and land. It is important to fully understand the weather patterns of the area a general plans to attack. The German attempt to push toward Moscow over the winter of 1941–1942 is often seen as a prime example of not understanding weather patterns. The German army was simply not equipped to handle a Russian winter and they suffered greatly because of the leaders' poor planning. It is just as important to understand the terrain that the army will need to traverse. Not only the distance to the enemy forces, but what the terrain looks like. Is it mountainous? Are there valleys? Will troops have to trudge through swampland? Is it wide-open space, or are there places for troops to easily hide? These are all questions a general must ask, and know the answers to, before engaging in battle.

The commander refers to the person leading the troops into battle. According Sun Tzu, the command must be wise, benevolent, sincere, courageous and strict. But it is more than that; Sun Tzu makes a specific distinction between the ruler and the commander and encourages the ruler not to interfere, saying:

He will win who has military capacity and is not interfered with by the sovereign.

The ruler is the one who engages in strategy, who is the voice of and to the people, and who makes the decisions, for the most part, about whom to attack. It is the commander that is responsible for the tactical. The commander ensures that the troops are in the right frame of mind, understands the strengths and weaknesses of the enemy, and plans the battle.

Finally, method and discipline describe the operations side of war. Commanders must ensure that the army is fed, that supply channels are kept clear, that supplies are properly distributed, that promotions and punishments are delivered, and all of the other issues involved in maintaining a well-run military. A well-maintained and disciplined army has a much better chance of succeeding in battle than does a poorly maintained and disciplined one.

Sun Tzu also recognized the importance of D&D in campaigns, writing:

All warfare is based on deception.
Hence, when able to attack, we must seem unable; when using our forces, we must seem inactive; when we are near, we must make the enemy believe we are far away; when far away, we must make him believe we are near.

These tactics are still in use today by military commanders and intelligence organizations around the world. Sun Tzu also focused on the other side of intelligence gathering: using indicators to detect enemy movements. With passages like:

The rising of birds in their flight is the sign of an ambuscade. Startled beads indicate that a sudden attack is coming.

Sun Tzu was helping commanders look at ways to determine the location of the enemy without being able to see them.

Sun Tzu also encouraged the use of spies in warfare, writing:

> *Thus, what enables the wise sovereign and the good general to strike and conquer, and achieve things beyond the reach of ordinary men, is foreknowledge.*

...

> *Hence it is only the enlightened ruler and the wise general who will use the highest intelligence of his army for the purposes of spying and thereby they achieve great results. Spies are a most important element in water, because on them depends an army's ability to move.*

Sun Tzu devotes an entire section to the discussion of spies, including recommending when to use spies, how to recruit local spies, how to convert enemy spies and delivering false information to known spies.

The Art of War is a short book (less than 60 pages) and an easy read. It is a worthwhile read and useful to think about how the steps outlined by Sun Tzu more than 2500 years ago are still relevant today.

JULIUS CAESAR

Julius Caesar is, without question, one of the greatest military leaders in the history of the world. His successes, combined with his tactical skill and decisiveness, has made him one of the most written about and studied military leaders in history. Although there is no denying that Caesar owes much his success to the strength of the Roman army, at the time the largest professional army the world had ever seen, in his writings he also attributed his success to intelligence gathering.

In his account of the Gallic war, *Commentaries on the Gallic War*, Caesar (1869) outlined his use of intelligence to better prepare for war with the different regions within Gaul.

> *Caesar, immediately learning this through his scouts, [but] fearing an ambuscade, because he had not yet discovered for what reason they were departing, kept his army and cavalry within the camp. At daybreak, the intelligence having been confirmed by the scouts, he sent forward his cavalry to harass their rear.*

Caesar was cautious, he confirmed his intelligence through multiple sources, whenever possible, and did not act until he was sure he has all of the information. *Commentaries on the Gallic War* is full of anecdotes of receiving reports from scouts and attempts to recruit spies from within the territories he was attempting to conquer.

Caesar instilled the important of tradecraft on his underlings. As with today's modern intelligence agencies, it was not enough to simply collect the information. For data to be considered intelligence it had to meet certain standards, Caesar emphasized the importance of weighing sources and understanding what information was trustworthy and what wasn't.

Caesar also used code to mask his communications. When communicating with Cicero during a war with Nervii, Caesar wrote:

Then with great rewards he induces a certain man of the Gallic horse to convey a letter to Cicero. This he sends written in Greek characters, lest the letter being intercepted, our measures should be discovered by the enemy. He directs him, if he should be unable to enter, to throw his spear with the letter fastened to the thong, inside the fortifications of the camp.

By communicating in Greek, Caesar was able to mask his communication. Sheldon postulates that Caesar also used a monoalphabetic cipher in communication. This means the communiqué would have been translated into Greek and the encoded on top of that (Sheldon, 2005).

Caesar also ran a network of spies within Rome, knowing that understanding what was happening within the city was just as important as what was going on in other countries. Unfortunately for Caesar, he did not receive the most important piece of intelligence in time. Caesar's network of spies within Rome had collected a list of conspirators against him within the Roman government. Caesar had the list, but had not read it when he was assassinated.

The one final intelligence lesson that can be learned from Caesar is that intelligence has a limited TTL. For intelligence to be effective, it must not only be produced and disseminated in a timely fashion, it also has to be read and acted on by the intelligence consumer. If each of these criteria is not met, then even the most important piece of intelligence is rendered useless.

GEORGE WASHINGTON

By the time the Revolutionary War started George Washington was no stranger to intelligence. He had served as a scout during the French and Indian War; therefore he was familiar with the benefits of a strong intelligence program. Washington took the lessons he learned during the French and Indian War to establish intelligence capabilities during the Revolutionary War (Walton, 2010b). In fact, Washington set up such a formalized system for intelligence collection and dissemination that he is known as the first Director of Central Intelligence.

Washington relied on intelligence out of necessity. He was facing a larger, well-trained force in his fight against the British and he knew he would need every advantage he could get. His network of spies throughout the colonies were useful not only for tracking the movement of British troops, but also as a conduit for feeding British Troops false information. Washington used his spies to run a number of successful D&D operations against the British.

The most famous spy network created by Washington was the Culper Spy Ring in New York. While Washington oversaw all intelligence activity during the Revolutionary War, he appointed Major Benjamin Tallmadge as the director of Military Intelligence in New York and instructed him to recruit spies. Tallmadge built a network of more than 20 spies in New York. This spy ring was known as the Culper Ring.

With Tallmadge serving as their case office, the agents in the Culper Ring reported to Tallmadge only, they did not know each other and they did not communicate with Washington – in fact, Washington did not know who the members of the Culper Ring were. Tallmadge, like Washington, used to identify members of the Culper Ring, he never used their real names in correspondence.

Washington and Tallmadge communicated using a simple code and each leader had a codebook. The code was a numeric substitution cipher wherein common words were replaced with numbers, for example *ally* was replaced with *25, general* with *235,* and *remittance* with *579.* There was also a facility to write out words that were not included in the original code using numerical cipher (Allen, 2004).

One reason why Washington was so successful is that he knew the right questions to ask. Washington's questions were insightful and detailed, and he would ask follow-up questions as needed. This level of specificity is critical to derive effective intelligence and is an area that intelligence consumers often fail at. Intelligence queries are similar to the old programming adage "garbage in, garbage out." If the right questions are not asked, it is impossible to get the right answer. It becomes incumbent on intelligence professionals to coach the consumers of intelligence to ask the right questions.

Although Washington did believe in the power of intelligence, he never established a formal counterintelligence program, nor did he centralize counterintelligence activities. Instead, he left this to the local commanders who were better equipped to not only gather intelligence through open sources (e.g. innkeepers and the like) but also were better able to identify loyalists and sympathizers to the crown in their own locales. Washington also created the Committee on Detecting and Defeating Conspiracies to close the channels of intelligence in New York, a place rife with Tory spies. John Jay was the first head of the Committee, which became the first counterespionage service in the United States. John Jay later became Chief Justice of the Supreme Court of the United States and was named the father of American counterintelligence by the CIA in 1997.

Washington established a professional intelligence organization that practiced rigorous tradecraft and distributed information on a need-to-know basis. Many of the techniques and methods used by Washington, though primitive, are still used by intelligence agencies today.

BLETCHLEY PARK

It is not hyperbole to say that without Bletchley Park, it is likely that World War II would have ended very differently. Winston Churchill famously said, "It was thanks to Ultra that we won the war." Bletchley Park's influence did not stop with World War II. The team at Bletchley Park has had a profound influence on intelligence agencies around the world and the American intelligence system is still modeled after team at Bletchley Park. In addition to policy, Bletchley Park has had great influence over the development of technology around the world for the last 70 years. During World War II, the goal of the team at Bletchley Park was to intercept and decode messages from the Axis forces. The team at Bletchley Park not only needed to intercept and transcribe messages, they also needed to be able to break the cipher that the Axis powers were using and get the data into the hands of consumers around the world in a timely manner.

They did this with stunning success. Their successes included breaking the Enigma cipher machine code and keeping the fact that the code had been broken a secret. Colossus, the world's first electronic computer, was also developed at Bletchley Park during World War II.

In the beginning, recruits to Bletchley Park had no idea what type of activity they would be engaging in and different teams were assigned to "huts," so that only a few people understood the entire operation (Hinsley and Stripp, 1993).

The process of intercepting transmissions, deciphering the transmissions and disseminating the data was given the codename Ultra. At its peak, the team at Bletchley Park was 8000 strong, about 80% of the workers were women, and deciphering about 4000 messages each day.

One of the biggest challenges faced by those at Bletchley Park was dissemination of information. There were a number of campaigns, such as the German offensive at Ardennes, that could have been dealt with more effectively had the intelligence gathered through Ultra been considered. Because the scope and nature of this type of collection was new to many Allied commanders, it was not always given the prominence it should have been in the analysts' production of FINTEL.

Commanders who were used to more traditional types of intelligence collection sources had an anchoring bias to those sources and gave them more weight. Fortunately, there were many Allied commanders who did not have this bias and those commanders were able to use data collected at Bletchley Park to launch more effective campaigns.

An early success of Ultra occurred in February 1941. Because of early decryption of Italian army ciphers, Ultra was able to provide information that led to the defeat of the Italian army in North Africa. In March 1941, through crypts collected and decrypted from Italian and German troops, the British navy knew that the Italians intended to attack convoys. The British turned the convoys around and launched an attack against the Italian navy in the Battle of Cape Mattapan. Thanks, in part, to the capabilities of Ultra, the British defeated the Italians and maintained control of the Mediterranean Sea.

CONCLUSION

The next chapter will start the focus on cyber threat intelligence, but it is important to understand that cyber threat intelligence is not an entirely new field. Instead, it is a field that builds on the thousands of years of accumulated wisdom surrounding intelligence. Many of the things Sun Tzu said about military intelligence 2500 years ago are relevant today both in traditional intelligence organizations and in cyber intelligence organizations.

Just as the leaders in Bletchley Park opened new avenues in intelligence collection, while still applying good tradecraft and adhering to the intelligence cycle, today's cyber threat intelligence teams are breaking new ground. The goal for these teams should be to continue to expand the realm of intelligence while drawing from history and adopting the best practices of a strong and successful intelligence organization.

REFERENCES

Allen, T.B., 2004. George Washington, Spymaster: How the Americans Outspied the British and Won the Revolutionary War. Thomas B Allen National Geographic Society, Washington, DC.

Bruce, J.B., Bennett, M., 2008. Foreign denial and deception: analytical imperatives. In: George, R.Z., Bruce, J.B. (Eds.), Analyzing Intelligence: Origins, Obstacles, and Innovations. Georgetown University Press, Washington, DC.

Caesar, J., 1869. Commentaries on the Gallic War Book II (W.A. McDevitte and W.S. Bohn, Trans.). Harper, New York.

Central Intelligence Agency (CIA), Office of Public Affairs, 1999. A Consumer's Guide to Intelligence. Central Intelligence Agency, Washington, DC, p. vii.

Davis, J., 2008. Why bad things happen to good analysts. In: George, R.Z., Bruce, J.B. (Eds.), Analyzing Intelligence: Origins, Obstacles, and Innovations. Georgetown University Press, Washington, DC.

Department of Defense (DOD), 2014. DOD dictionary of military and associated terms "intelligence". <http://www.dtic.mil/doctrine/dod_dictionary/data/i/4850.html> (accessed 15.06.14.).

Erskine, R., Smith, M. (Eds.), 2011. The Bletchley Park Codebreakers (Dialogue Espionage Classics). Biteback Publishing, London.

Federal Bureau of Investigation (FBI), Directorate of Intelligence, 2014. Intelligence defined. <http://www.fbi.gov/about-us/intelligence/defined> (accessed 16.07.14.).

Gill, P., Phythian, M., 2012. Intelligence in an Insecure World, second ed. Polity, New York, p. 7.

Hinsley, F.H., Stripp, A. (Eds.), 1993. Codebreakers: The Inside Story of Bletchley Park. Oxford University Press, New York.

Sheldon, R.M., 2005. Intelligence Activities in Ancient Rome: Trust in the Gods But Verify. Routledge, New York, p. 126.

Tzu, S., 2012a. The Art of War, (Lionel Giles, Trans.). Polity, New York, p. 11.

Tzu, S., 2012b. The Art of War (Lionel Giles, Trans.). Polity, New York, p. 3.

Walton, T., 2010a. The fall of the shah. Challenges in Intelligence Analysis: Lessons from 1300 BCE to the Present. Cambridge University Press, New York, pp. 183-187.

Walton, T., 2010b. George Washington. Challenges in Intelligence Analysis: Lessons from 1300 BCE to the Present. Cambridge University Press, New York, pp. 55-59.

Warner, M., 2007. Wanted: a definition of "intelligence": understanding our craft. <https://www.cia.gov/library/center-for-the-study-of-intelligence/csi-publications/csi-studies/studies/vol46no3/article02.html> (accessed 16.07.14.).

Building a network security intelligence model

## 3

INFORMATION IN THIS CHAPTER:

- Defining Cyber Threat Intelligence
- The Anatomy of an Attack
- Approaching Cyber Attacks Differently
- Incorporating the Intelligence Lifecycle into Security Workflow
- Automation

INTRODUCTION

A traditional intelligence organization requires dozens, if not hundreds or thousands, of people to run effectively. There are whole organizations built around collection, processing, analysis, and dissemination, and an often impenetrable management chain assigned to planning and direction.

That is not the case with the network security team at most organizations. According to a Ponemon Institute survey of 504 large organizations, the average size of a security team was 22 people in 2013, with that number expected to grow to 29 in 2014 (Ponemon Institute, 2014). Of course, those are large organizations; medium and small organizations have a considerably smaller staff. Which begs the question: How can a resource-constrained network security staff possibly hope to use intelligence to improve security?

The simple fact is, there is no alternative. Threats against the network are growing too rapidly and the attack surface is expanding too quickly for traditional security measures to continue to be effective, as they exist today. Combine these two facts with the fact that very few organizations are increasing their network security budget at the rate they should. There needs to be an effective way to introduce cyber threat intelligence into an organization, make existing systems more effective while improving the intelligence tradecraft of the security team.

DEFINING CYBER THREAT INTELLIGENCE

In Chapter 2 (see page 0000), the definition for intelligence was introduced as:

Intelligence is the umbrella term referring to the range of activities – from planning and information collection to the analysis and dissemination – conducted in secret and aimed at maintaining or enhancing relative security by providing forewarning of threats or potential threats in a manner that allows for the timely implementation of a preventive policy or strategy, including, where deemed desirable, covert activities.

That is a pretty good start to defining cyber threat intelligence. Gartner (McMillan, 2013) uses the following definition instead:

Evidence-based knowledge, including context, mechanisms, indicators, implications and actionable advice, about an existing or emerging menace or hazard to assets that can be used to inform decisions regarding the subject's response to that menace or hazard.

For the purposes of this book this definition works very well because it includes all aspects of cyber threat intelligence that are critical to a security team's success.

Similar to the traditional definition of intelligence, the cyber threat intelligence definition focuses on the fact that intelligence should be actionable. Especially in smaller shops, cyber threat intelligence needs to present itself in the form of an immediate action that the security team can take to protect the network.

The other aspect of this definition that is important, and missing from the original definition outlined in chapter 2, is the emphasis on context. There are really two areas where context comes into play. First, a network threat is not really a threat if the target network is not susceptible to it. Context is critical in the realm of cyber threat intelligence, it is not enough to know what threats are out there, an effective security organization also must have a complete understanding of the assets within the larger organization that that they are protecting. Second, it is important to understand the context of the threat itself. Is it a Distributed Denial of Service (DDoS) attack coming from an unfocused group that launches a DDoS attack against one organization and quickly moves on, or is it from a well-organized team that uses DDoS attacks to mask other activity?

This a good place to make distinction regarding terminology. The terms *vulnerability, exploit,* and *threat* often overlap each other, but each term has a specific meaning that will be used throughout this book. A vulnerability is a weakness in an application, system, or process that can be used to gain increased access, disrupt normal use, or other for other potentially malicious action. An exploit is either automated code or manual action that can be taken to leverage the exposure created by a vulnerability. A threat is the availability of a specific vulnerability within an organization's network that has the potential to subject to be exploited. Threats and exploits are active while vulnerabilities are passive.

A point that has been made before but bears repeating in light of this definition is this: Intelligence is not data. Until collected data has been put through the analysis process, either internally or through a third party, it is just information. It is only after collections have gone through the intelligence lifecycle that they become intelligence. The definition includes mention of indicators. In the realm of cyber threat intelligence an indicator is usually an IP address, domain, file hash, Registry entry, signature, or something along those line. By themselves, those indicators are not intelligence. Indicators must be combined with knowledge about those indicators, the level of threat they pose to the target network, and their relevance to the target network before they become intelligence.

For example, there are a number of sources (some used later in this book) that provide lists of IP addresses for use in protecting the network. Those IP address lists, by themselves, are not intelligence. Instead, those IP addresses become intelligence when they are detected inside a network or in a similar network. Only when those IP addresses become actionable – for example, a blocked threat – do they turn from information into potential intelligence.

THE ANATOMY OF AN ATTACK

To develop better tradecraft for dealing with cyber attacks, it is important to first understand how an attack works and distinguish between different types of attacks. The methods outlined in this chapter and throughout the book are not designed to deal with one-off attacks or widespread attacks that cast a large net and have no real thought behind them. The tools most security teams have today deal with those attacks very effectively because those attacks use commodity malware and are designed to be delivered en masse with no concept of targeting.

The discussion around the use of intelligence to detect and prevent cyber attacks is specifically referring to attacks that are planned and targeted. Recall that security companies saw a significant increase in targeted attacks in 2013, and Symantec has reported that 1 in 5.2 small business and 1 in 2.3 large enterprises were subject to targeted attacks. By all estimations the number of targeted attacks will continue to grow. Targeted attacks are not just the realm of the advanced persistent threat (APT) any more. In fact, as the underground market continues to expand and more cyber criminals are improving their tradecraft, distinguishing a targeted attack from an APT is becoming more difficult. Of course, whether an attack is an APT or a run-of-the-mill targeted attack is irrelevant, stopping it is what matters. To do that security teams must think like an attacker and understand how the intrusion process works.

Lockheed Martin developed the attack chain model shown in Figure 3.1 (Hutchins et al, n.d.) on behalf of the Department of Defense. It lays out seven parts to a typical targeted attack, each one moving closer to gaining access to the network.

The first step in any targeted attack is reconnaissance. Five years ago reconnaissance of a targeted network involved scanning public-facing IP addresses looking for vulnerable systems. Today, there still may be some of that, but it is not nearly as critical to the success of the operation. Instead, modern reconnaissance involves scanning social media accounts, scraping LinkedIn, looking at conference websites and even just a routine Google search for "@targetdomain.com."

In fact, most reconnaissance operations can be conducted without ever touching the targeted organization's network. There is a treasure trove of information available through search engines, mining mailing list archives, and using networking tools available through the American Registry for Internet Numbers (ARIN) or the

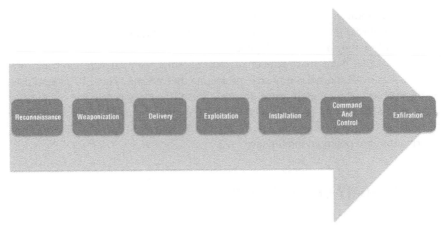

FIGURE 3.1

The attack chain.

regional equivalent's Web site. Should actually touching the target network with a scan become necessary, it is easy to redirect that activity through a compromised host or through rented hosting infrastructure purchased with a prepaid (or stolen) credit card. Not that it matters. Organizations are scanned by hundreds or thousands of IP addresses each day, so it is very rare to find an organization that retains that information.

Once the reconnaissance phase of the operation is complete, the next phase is weaponization. In this phase, the attacker joins a remote access tool (RAT) with an exploit and determines the method of delivery. In most cases, the delivery will be via email and the exploitation will occur via a Web site or a compromised document. When a Web site is used it will either be a Web site specifically set up by the attacker for this operation (though, if successful, the Web site may be reused) or it will be a link to a legitimate Web site that the attacker has compromised – often introducing a weaponized banner ad into the site's rotation.

The third step in the attack is delivery of the weaponized tool using the chosen delivery method. This is the launch of the email attack, start of the social media campaign, or activating the weaponized tool in a compromised Web site used as a watering hole. The delivery portion of the campaign can take anywhere from a few days to several weeks. During this time the attackers continue to refine and improve their delivery methods so as to improve their rates of success. If this sounds similar to a discussion the marketing department might have, it is. Just as marketing teams review successes and failures, so do attackers during an operation. They will try different mail messages, track which messages were read, which weren't read and make adjustments to improve the number of hits they receive.

The next step in the chain is the actual exploitation, the tool is delivered and the target clicks on the link, opens the file or plugs in the USB drive and something on the target system is exploited. That exploit could be of an application on the system such as Adobe Acrobat or Internet Explorer or it could be an exploitation of the operating system itself. It also could be an exploitation of the target itself. Many effective campaigns have relied on simply popping a message on the target's screen reading, "In order to view this video you need to download a new driver," or a similar message. Another common tactic to trick targets is for attackers to pretend to be network administrators and tell the target they need to establish a remote session to their machine. The job of the attacker is a lot simpler with a willing target.

Most attackers use a two-stage stage system. The exploit will contain a loader, which is a very small, memory-resident, application that is used to download and install the actual RAT. These loaders stay memory resident because they are less likely to be detected by traditional security tools, such as antivirus software, and the loader can initiate a quick scan of the system and decide which RAT will be installed on the system.

Installation is the fifth stage in the attack chain. Every attacker has two or three favorite tools the attacker uses to gain remote access to the network. Most RATs do more than just communicate out; they are extensible, allowing the attacker to install tools such as a key logger, screen grabber, network scanner, or whatever else is needed. RATs are used on a per-operation basis. That doesn't mean that the same RAT is not used from one operation to another; rather that the attacker will recompile the RAT between operations (sometimes even within the same operation) so that it looks completely different to antivirus tools. It will still perform the same functions, but the antivirus tool will not know it is the same program.

The next step in the attack chain is command and control (C&C). The installed RAT will attempt to call out to the attacker's infrastructure and gain command-line access to the victim machines. There is usually a waiting period while the RAT sleeps, and then it will call out to an IP address, domain name, or URL. The most common port used for communication between the RAT and the C&C host is port 80 (HTTP), although port 443 (HTTPS) is becoming increasingly common. Gone are the days when attackers would use ports that were easy to block, such as 6666 and 6667 (IRC) or 21 (FTP); HTTP traffic is ubiquitous in networks and it is easy to blend in with other traffic using HTTP and the C&C protocol.

Once the attacker gains access, the attacker must survey the system as well as the internal network looking for more vulnerable hosts to which to spread the attack. Sometimes this is by design. The initial entry point may not be of particular interest so the attacker will use it to gain a foothold in the network, compromise other machines, and remove signs of entry from the original box. This way, even if the intrusion is discovered later, the original entry point and means of access is hidden from the security team and can be successfully used again, if needed. This is part of the exfiltration step in the attack chain. Once in the attacker will conduct network discovery, review files on the machine and the rest of the network and grab everything that will help them reach their objective.

This highlights another important way that the attack landscape has changed over the last few years: just as intelligence organizations have customers who put in collection requests and receive finished intelligence (FINTEL), so do the attackers. In fact, those attackers may be part of a private or state-sponsored intelligence organization that is fulfilling requests from their leaders. Sophisticated attackers often use the same intelligence lifecycle as the organizations they are targeting. Which means, in many ways, the attackers are more sophisticated than the organizations that they are targeting.

APPROACHING CYBER ATTACKS DIFFERENTLY

That attackers often operate in a more sophisticated manner than the organizations they are targeting means that, to be effective, security teams in those organizations must change the way they approach security. Switching from the current model of "Whack-a-Mole" security, where security teams respond to every threat as it "pops up" (pardon the pun), without having any context as to the true nature of the threat will not work against a sophisticated adversary. By using the intelligence lifecycle outlined in Chapter 2 (see page 0000), security teams become more efficient and can more effectively block the threats that post the most danger to an organization.

The way most organizations today are structured, if an attacker is caught at all, it will be during step 6 or 7 of the attack chain; that is during the C&C or exfiltration step. Unfortunately, as exemplified by the spate of high-profile data breaches in 2013 and 2014, that is too late.

For security teams to become more effective, they must adopt an intelligence-led model of network security, often referred to as Intelligence-Guided Computer Network Defense (IGCND). Using intelligence from external sources and intelligence collected internally, security teams can detect more attacks earlier in the attack chain, thus improving effectiveness and providing better protection to the organization's assets.

How can intelligence help to improve the effectiveness of a security team and stop attacks earlier in the attack chain? By providing relevant information to the right people, at the right time, enabling them to take action in a timely manner. Just as the dedicated men and women at Bletchley Park (see Chapter 2, page 0000) built a new collection system that permanently changed the way intelligence is gathered, so are the network security teams building intelligence-led security programs.

To begin moving toward an intelligence-led security program, security teams need to start assessing the intelligence they already have, dividing it up based on the intelligence pyramid shown in Figure 3.2. Intelligence should be divided into strategic, tactical, and operational, and delivered to the team in need of that specific type of intelligence.

Strategic intelligence is intelligence for those at the highest levels of the organization. It is designed to help senior management understand the big picture surrounding the threats to an organization and budget to protect against those threats appropriately. Strategic intelligence should focus on answering the big questions: Who, Why, and Where. Who are the adversary groups targeting the organization? Why are they

FIGURE 3.2

The intelligence pyramid.

are targeting the organization? and Where else have they launched attacks? Depending on the nature of the attack and the tradecraft of the adversaries, these can be easy questions to answer or next to impossible.

In some ways, the increase in so-called hactivism style attacks makes the job of security teams easier. By monitoring Twitter, Pastebin, and other well-known resources, it is trivial to discover which organizations are being targeted by DDoS or other hacking campaigns at any given time. Irrespective of the effectiveness of these campaigns, it is a good practice for organizations to maintain information about the different campaigns targeting them. It does not have to be anything fancy, an Excel spreadsheet will do, as long as it is accessible to all the people who may need it. Tracking these types of campaigns provides an easy entry into the world of collecting strategic intelligence, but it only provides a small part of the picture.

Attackers who are not looking to score points and prove a point to their followers on Twitter are much more difficult to track. Generally, organizations will need third-party assistance to find out who is behind the campaigns and what is motivating them. After all, if a group is targeting one organization in chances are they have targeted another. So another organization is familiar with the adversary and its motivation. Motivation is an important factor in an attack. Not in the psychological sense of "I hack networks because I was picked last in gym class," but in the sense of determining what information the adversary is after. Some attackers are interested in credit card or personally identifiable information (PII) data, others are interested in blueprints and formulas, some are interested in information or reporting and some are interested in using a smaller organization to gain access to a larger one. There are myriad motivations behind campaigns and knowing what type of information an adversary is looking for helps guide the security team as to where to allocate resources.

To effectively gauge what data is of value within the organization, the security team must engage in counterintelligence. A key aspect of counterintelligence is to develop a strategic profile of the organization. Knowing the high-value items that exist within the organization that make it a potential victim is of significant importance to leaders at this level. By maintaining this repository of strategic targeting information, the security team knows, as the organization shifts global policy, how it may affect the campaigns and groups to which the organization are exposed at a high level.

If strategic intelligence is designed for company leaders, then leaders on the security team use tactical intelligence. Tactical intelligence answers what and when questions by providing information about adversaries tactics, techniques, and procedures (TTPs). For lack of a better term, an adversary's TTPs are its signature. TTPs help to identify an adversary behind an attack by isolating unique patterns of attack behavior. For example, an adversary may only engage in attack activity Monday through Friday from 9:00 AM to 5:00 PM Moscow time. As has been mentioned before, most adversaries will have a few favorite toolsets that they reuse. Adversaries generally prefer one attack vector to another; some attackers prefer spear-phishing campaigns, whereas others prefer watering holes. An adversary may have a penchant for certain exploits, or type of exploits. There are a host of different attributes that these adversaries use, that not only become crutches but also help identify them to their targets. Especially in cases when the adversary is revisiting a target.

Operational intelligence within the realm of cyber security is geared toward, unsurprisingly, the operators. Operational intelligence generally consists of indicators of compromise (IOCs) that firewall, Intrusion Detection System (IDS), mail server, and proxy administrators can use to better protect the organization's network. IOCs are artifacts, such as IP addresses, domain names, file hashes, and Registry entries, that are indicative of an attack. IOCs are also useful for incident response (IR) teams, so they can react more quickly to an outbreak or suspected intrusion.

A NOTE ABOUT TIME TO LIVE

For intelligence to be effective, it has to be disseminated to the right people within the organization. Handing the chief information security officer (CISO) a bunch of IP addresses is not as effective as handing the firewall administrator those IP addresses. The firewall administrator will be able to make more immediate use of that data.

In addition to ensuring information is disseminated to the right consumer, it is important that intelligence be delivered in a timely manner. Intelligence that could have prevented a breech doesn't do anyone good if it is delivered to the security team three days after the attack.

Generally speaking, the higher intelligence is on the intelligence pyramid, the longer that intelligence is useful before it expires, in other words it has a longer time to live (TTL). This makes sense, adversary groups are somewhat static – members may come and go, but the group remains intact and conducts attacks on a regular basis. That doesn't mean that adversaries don't disband (or get arrested), but those are longer-term trends. Similarly, an adversary does not often change its TTPs; they tend to stick with the same tools and methods across the lifecycle of the group. Occasionally, TTPs do change. As an adversary matures they may acquire new capabilities, or a favorite tool gets exposed by a security vendor (by sheer coincidence, usually around the time of a major security conference) and falls out of use. But those events tend to be infrequent within the lifespan of an adversary.

Operational intelligence generally has a very short TTL. An IP address engaged in malicious activity right now may no longer be compromised in a few hours. Domains used to launch spear-phishing attacks may no longer be used in a few days, and a file hash that is being used as a payload in a watering hole attack may no longer be used in a few weeks.

It is important to keep these TTLs in mind when delivering intelligence (Figure 3.3). Operational intelligence must be vetted and delivered as quickly as possible. That does mean that operation intelligence is also subject to more false-positives than other types of intelligence, but speed is paramount. Strategic and tactical intelligence have a longer shelf life, so these types of FINTEL should be better researched and delivered with a higher level of confidence. That is not to say that speed and efficiency are not important when it comes to strategic and tactical intelligence, they most certainly are. But in the case of these types of intelligence, accuracy and detailed analysis is more important than speed.

It is important to keep in mind which group, or groups, within an organization need the different types of intelligence within an organization. Every organization is different and manages security differently, so the teams who have a need to know will vary. Getting the flow of information correct while developing an intelligence team will improve the process of getting FINTEL into the hands of the people who need it.

It is important to note here that leaders at the top of organizations often believe that they need operational or tactical intelligence. Providing that type of intelligence

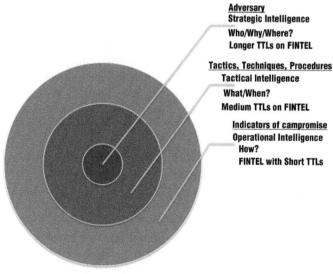

Adversary
Strategic Intelligence
Who/Why/Where?
Longer TTLs on FINTEL

Tactics, Techniques, Procedures
Tactical Intelligence
What/When?
Medium TTLs on FINTEL

Indicators of campromise
Operational Intelligence
How?
FINTEL with Short TTLs

FIGURE 3.3

Intelligence types and TTLs.

may not only be confusing to them, but also slow down the availability of this intelligence to the defensive operators if they have to prepare reporting to the strategic leadership that focuses on the operational intelligence. Instead combinations of operational indicators and tactical intelligence should be provided to strategic staff members as part of the After Action Report (AAR) of events for inclusion in their overall strategic intelligence planning.

INCORPORATING THE INTELLIGENCE LIFECYCLE INTO SECURITY WORKFLOW

For many organizations creating and continuously running an intelligence cycle seems like a daunting task. The truth is, most security teams are already engaged in activities that mirror the intelligence lifecycle and don't realize it. Very few security vendors don't deliver at least some form of rudimentary intelligence into their products today. But, like the logs from the myriad of security tools, that intelligence is fragmented and not connected to other activities in the network.

Using intelligence that already exists within the network is a good start to building an intelligence lifecycle. By taking intelligence received from one vendor and disseminating that intelligence to other security systems within the network an organization can start to develop a crude intelligence lifecycle.

To take the intelligence lifecycle to the next level, the first thing an organization needs to do is step back and determine what is the mission, or missions, of the security team. The mission is not "to protect the network" or "keep hackers out." Those are examples of side effects of the true mission. To determine what the true mission is, an organization has to decide what its most valuable assets are: Is it a customer database, the formula for a perfect burrito, blueprints for new type of plane, or the people within the organization? Once the leadership has identified the most valuable assets then a mission can be created. That mission should be explicitly stated: *"The mission of the security team is to protect our client data, including personally identifiable information, as well as data from customer credit card transactions."*

Notice that the mission is both explicit and actionable in that it allows the security team to focus resources appropriately. There can be more than one mission running simultaneously, and most of the time there will be several concurrent missions, but leadership needs to set the priorities of those missions, and both the missions and their priority level need to be evaluated periodically to ensure they still make sense. This can be done as part of the annual program assessment of the security organization, or any time a major shift in business practices, priorities, or tactics is imminent (e.g. a forthcoming merger and acquisition or global expansion).

After the mission has been defined, the next step is to direct the security team to collect data in support of that mission. Using the example mission above, to start the collection process the security team will first need to understand what systems within the organization collect customer data and are involved in the processing of credit card transactions. This is a key step and one that is often overlooked: It is impossible to protect a system when it is not fully understood.

After the customer databases and credit card processing systems are fully accounted for, the security team can pull log data and review security incidents related to those systems from the past few months. In addition, if one has not already been done, the security team can run a vulnerability scan against those systems to find known vulnerabilities. If these systems are to be protected from the adversary it is important to know what their weaknesses are, so they can either be patched or protected in some other way.

After all of the internal data on the systems has been gathered the next step is to begin the external search. External searches should involve reaching out to the organization's security vendors, using search engines, and collecting information from intelligence providers and vertical associations, such as Information Sharing and Analysis Centers (ISACs). Just as the mission has to be actionable, when querying each of these sources, it is important to ask the right questions: "What adversary groups are most active selling PII data in the underground market?" "What adversary groups are associated with these artifacts discovered in the network?" or "Who are the latest groups targeting our specific vertical?" Each of these sources is a good collection point. Most organizations are not going to create their own collection systems for cyber intelligence data, there simply are not enough resources available to do that. Instead, the collection process will most likely rely heavily on information from trusted third-party sources.

So far, no intelligence has been produced. All that has been done to this point is data gathering. The next step is to take the collected data and process it. Processing can be done manually, but that is a lengthy and painful process. Most organizations use a Security Information and Event Management (SIEM) for compliance and security purposes. A SIEM can also serve as a repository for externally collected data. Using a SIEM to store collected data has the benefit of integrating the cyber threat intelligence lifecycle into existing workflows. Rather than completely changing how security is handled within the organization, making modifications to existing processes will allow the organization to enhance security by creating an intelligence overlay using the lifecycle model.

Not every organization has a SIEM in place. In those cases, something will need to be developed that will allow the security team to correlate internal and external information to produce intelligence. Some organizations are doing this today with object-oriented databases such as Palantir or Apache's Hadoop. This does require more time to set up and it is a new process that will need to be attended to, but given the volume of security data, internal and external, that an organization of any size can collect, there needs to be a processing system in place to support the load.

The next phase of the intelligence lifecycle is the analysis phase, it is here that all of the data collected internally and externally is finally turned into intelligence. Some of the collected data may be able to be quickly turned into FINTEL. For example, a report from a trusted source indicates that the hacker group Deep Panda is planning to launch attacks against similar organizations. If the veracity of the report is verified, it quickly becomes strategic intelligence, and accompanying the report should be any information from the first source, or others, about the TTPs of Deep Panda; that becomes tactical intelligence. Finally, if Deep Panda has launched successful attacks against similar organizations, information surrounding the IOCs that were used in those attacks becomes operational intelligence.

Once the intelligence is produced it should be disseminated and there should be feedback from the various consumers as to its effectiveness. Perhaps word comes from the operations teams that one of the IP addresses that was reported to have been used by Deep Panda in another attack showed up in a firewall log as successfully blocked, but a file hash matching one discovered on a compromised network is found on the desktop of someone in Human Resources. Obviously, in that scenario, there is immediate need for the Incident Response team. However, there also needs to be an AAR on the part of the analysis team updating the intelligence to reflect the suspected intrusion.

INTELLIGENCE IS ALIVE

With respect to Dr Frankenstein, even though it may be cobbled together from bits and pieces of information from a variety of sources, once something becomes FINTEL it is now a living document. That means it needs to be continuously updated and, as with software, it needs to have a version number and published date attached to it, so consumers can always be sure they are reviewing the most recent version.

Updates are especially important to IOCs, because of their short lifespan. Often, rather than push updated FINTEL for IOCs, analysts will assign a TTL to the indicators when they are published. Alternatively, some security teams just push out a new set of indicators each day, with the explication being that operational teams will discard the previous day's indicators. This allows the analysts on the security team to track TTLs internally without having to share that information throughout the organization and helps to reduce the number of false positives.

Of course it is not just operational intelligence that needs to be updated; changes happen across the full spectrum of intelligence. Both strategically and tactically, changes in intelligence can have a significant impact on the focus and resource allocation of an organization. For example, if an organization was targeted by TeslaTeam in the past and has devoted resources to protections specifically designed to combat the TTPs in use by TeslaTeam, finding out that the membership of TeslaTeam is on the wane, as is their effectiveness, would allow those resources to be allocated other places.

By maintaining a true cyber threat intelligence lifecycle an organization will have immediate and current information surrounding the threats that are most relevant to it and know what their security threat landscape looks like at any given time.

A PICTURE IS WORTH A THOUSAND WORDS

As a security team and the larger organization mature their security approach from "Whack-a-Mole" to one that is intelligence-led, it is important to think about ways to visualize data. Like it or not the Internet acronym TL;DR (Too Long; Didn't Read) holds true in corporate environments. For every leader who appreciates well-thought-out analytical content in strategic reports, there are many more who don't have the time to read it.

To overcome the disdain for reading shown by many leaders, security teams have devised a number of ways to communicate intelligence to leaders that is eye catching, easy to comprehend, and gets the point across. A visualization tool can be something as simple as a dashboard that displays a red, yellow, or green icon showing the level of danger. However, the more detailed visualizations are often more effective at generating conversations that lead to deeper understanding of the threats and produce more intelligence requirements.

For example, instead of simply releasing a strategic report around a new threat, as well as reports that provide tactical and operational intelligence, some organizations will also include visualization. The visualization can look like a flow chart, with the name of the adversary, along with any known members at the top. Below the adversary are separate boxes to indicate the different types of TTPs associated with the adversary. One box might have the C&C tools they use, another box might describe preferred exploits, and so on. The third row would contain the IOCs associated with the specific TTPs. If the IP address or domain of the C&C server is known, it would be listed connected to the C&C slot in the tactical row.

Figure 3.4 is a representation of this type of flowchart, this one documenting a specific attack. It shows the adversary at the top and then describes the specific type of attack, along with related domains. On the left side of the chart it lists the victims, along with how they were exploited and what root kit was used. Below the exploit and the rootkit are listed the C&C hosts, and to the right of the root kit are listed additional victims who were exploited by the attacker after the initial breach.

Presenting a visual representation of the attack in this format can help security teams connect dots that may have been missed during the initial triage. While it may seem odd to turn the Security Operations Center into the board room from *The Wire*, it can be a very effective tool.

Creating the visualization makes the intelligence immediately accessible to executives who may only have a limited understanding of the technical aspects of the attack.

Visualization not only helps make intelligence more accessible, it can also help make connections that might have gone unnoticed. For example, plotting out spear-phishing attacks across a six-month period might show flows in the rates of attack that can help the mail administrators better prepare for future attacks, or even pinpoint when to send out reminder notifications to employees to watch out for phishing emails.

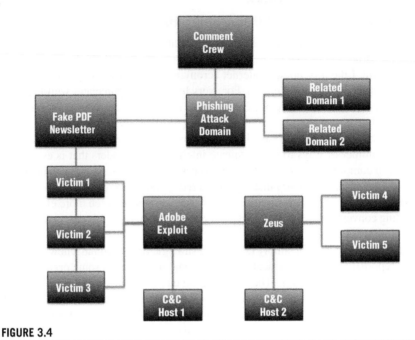

FIGURE 3.4

A flowchart representation of an attack.

Using graphs and other visual tools can also help change the conversation with the leadership of the organization. Too often security teams speak in terms of attacks identified or IP addresses blocked, terms that have no real meaning to the leadership of the organization. By using the right visual tools, the security team can communicate the value they provide to the organization in a way that a nontechnical leadership can easily understand. This should also include some form of information on the overall security and success of the business. A key issue here for any security team is showing value back to the business, whether that is in terms of fines prevented by attacks thwarted or revenue generated through minimization of downtime from disruptive attacks.

AUTOMATION

Large organizations receive thousands of security alerts, across all systems, every day. Even medium and small organizations can receive dozens or hundreds of alerts. Whatever the number, it is too many to track down and effectively handle. As an organization builds an intelligence-led security program the data overload will get worse.

Security and intelligence automation is a critical component of a successful intelligence-led security program. The underlying systems must be in place to automate the flow of data from direction to collection to processing to analyzing to dissemination and back to direction.

Building automation into the security lifecycle does not necessarily require new tools, but it does require cooperation between all teams within an organization and vendors outside that organization. To start, data that is needed for effective security analysis must be automatically collected in one place, whether that is a SIEM, an object-oriented database, or even a central syslog server, there has to be a single place to send data.

Data does not just mean log data, though that is a big chunk of it. Data is anything that is relevant to effective security analysis. That data could be regular updates of new hires and terminations, it could be information about new marketing campaigns, conference attendance and speaking roles for employees, and much more. Anything that could be relevant to the security of the organization, based on the previously defined missions, should be automatically delivered to a central repository.

Next, data from external sources needs to be automatically delivered to that same central repository. External data could include intelligence delivered via email, logs from cloud providers, or data feeds of external intelligence.

Collections themselves should also be automated. Whether the collection system is a programmed Google News alert, the results of an automated scraping of certain keywords on Twitter or Facebook, automated monitoring of an IRC channel, or data collection, those collections should automatically run and deliver the results into the same centralized repository.

Once data is delivered it needs to be automatically normalized. Data from different sources will be delivered in different formats. To effectively analyze the collected data, there needs to be a common framework encapsulating that data. This process is often called extract, transform, load (ETL) and can be best done by collaboration between the organization's data warehouse owner and the information experts. Meta data layers on top of the data are key to creating system usable by analysts for report synthesis. It does not matter what the framework is, as long as it is broad enough that it can include many different types of data and allow the different datasets to be correlated against each other.

Analysts must also have automated tools that allow them to query the central repository in a manner that is fast, but complete. Analysts can then automate queries that align with current intelligence missions and produce FINTEL in a timely manner. If the underlying systems do allow for successful querying across all forms of data, not only will analysts be able to produce timely reports, but also those reports will be more complete.

Dissemination should also be automated. Delivery of FINTEL should be accomplished through the click of a button, which would automatically distribute the reports to the right people. Although the analyst needs to be aware of who is receiving FINTEL to ensure they have a need to know, that does not mean the analyst should be looking through the organization's address book and deciding who should get it. There should be premade distribution lists. The analyst does not need to know each member of a specific distribution list, only that the list receives certain types of intelligence.

Feedback should also be automated; the delivered FINTEL should include a mechanism for requesting follow up information or providing feedback on the FIN-TEL. Just as getting executives to read reporting can be a challenge, so, too, can getting follow-up questions or additional requirements. Including the mechanism for feedback within the FINTEL itself expedites the feedback process and encourages more consumer participation.

Taking automation to the next level can include automating the process of ingesting IOCs into security systems. This is a patently ridiculous notion to many security professionals for reasons that are completely understandable. However, a happy side effect of building an intelligence-led security team is that it engenders trust between teams. Once that trust has been fully realized, and teams have more faith in each other, it makes sense to take a subset of high-confidence IOCs and automate delivery of that intelligence directly into the security systems that will benefit from them. This is not a trust that happens overnight, or even over a period of months. It takes time to develop confidence in the process and the people doing the analyzing. But the potential gain once that trust is earned far outweighs any misgivings skeptics within the organization may have.

One final note on automation: Automation does not mean hands off. The people involved in the intelligence lifecycle must be actively engaged in the process in order for it to be effective. The collection team must ensure they are running the correct queries in the right places and must always be looking for new avenues from which to collect. The processing team must ensure the data is delivered in proper format to the central repository and must monitor the integrity of the data. They must also take notice when a system, or systems, stops sending data to the central repository and track down why that is occurring. Analysts must regularly review their queries to make sure that the results are expected and touching all sources in the repository. Analysts must also review the feedback from the intelligence consumers to verify that the FINTEL is in line with what the client expected, that it answers the question asked. When FINTEL delivered to the consumer does produce new intelligence requirements, the intelligence leadership team must review those requests before passing them on to the collections team.

Automation, when done correctly, can improve the quality of the entire intelligence lifecycle while at the same time speeding up the process of collection, processing, analyzing and disseminating new intelligence. Although automation is a necessity in today's world of bombardment by cyber attacks, it cannot be the sole focus of the intelligence lifecycle. Proper oversight and review is necessary to make sure automated systems are delivering good data that will provide solid intelligence.

CONCLUSION

Building upon thousands of years of intelligence tradition today's security teams can create an intelligence-led security program. An intelligence-led security program is one that, according to Gartner, uses "…evidence-based knowledge, including context, mechanisms, indicators, implications and actionable advice, about an existing or emerging menace or hazard to assets that can be used to inform decisions regarding the subject's response to that menace or hazard."

By molding existing security systems using an intelligence lifecycle model an organization can become more efficient and respond to security events faster, which means stopping the attack earlier in the attack chain and better protecting the organizations most valuable assets.

The next section takes a look at how an organization does that and help answer a number of important questions, such as: What is needed for a security team to collect the right data from the right sources inside and outside the network and turn that data into actionable intelligence for use by the rest of the organization? More importantly, how does the security team, with very limited resources do all of that in an automated fashion without sacrificing security?

REFERENCES

Hutchins, E.M., Cloppert, M.J., Amin, R.M., n.d. Intelligence-driven computer network defense informed by analysis of adversary campaigns and intrusion kill chains. <http://www.lockheedmartin.com/content/dam/lockheed/data/corporate/documents/LM-White-Paper-Intel-Driven-Defense.pdf> (accessed 27.07.14.).

McMillan, R., 2013. Definition: threat intelligence. <https://www.gartner.com/doc/2487216/definition-threat-intelligence> (accessed 27.07.14.).

Ponemon Institute, 2014. Understaffed and at risk: today's IT security department. <http://www.hp.com/hpinfo/newsroom/press_kits/2014/RSAConference2014/Ponemon_IT_Security_Jobs_Report.pdf> (accessed 27.07.14.).

Gathering data

## 4

INFORMATION IN THIS CHAPTER:

- The Continuous Monitoring Framework
- NIST Cyber Security Framework
- Security + Intelligence
- The Business Side of Security
- Planning a Phased Approach

INTRODUCTION

The first section of this book was primarily theory-focused. Understanding the history of intelligence and creating a framework, like the intelligence cycle, in which to work is important for the rest of the book. None of that information actually helps an organization make the move from "Whack-a-Mole" security to building an intelligence-led security program. That is the focus of this section of the book.

Before diving in, it is important to set a baseline of the security program at a typical organization. Today, most security organizations work in the following manner: An alert pops up in a console (whether it is an antivirus console, firewall console, or Intrusion Detection System [IDS] console), the security team sees the alert and responds to the incident. That response may involve blocking an IP address in the firewall, updating an IDS signature, adding a domain to the block list on the proxy, or wiping an infected machine and restoring it from backup.

These methods are actually effective in stopping 80–85% of attacks against an organization and 10 years ago that would have been an acceptable level of protection. The problem today is that the undetected 15–20% of attacks are costing organizations millions of dollars in downtime and lost revenue. A missed attack can result in millions of credit cards being leaked to the underground, the plans for the next generation of your flagship product winding up in the hands of your competitor, or even all of your embarrassing executive emails leaked to Gawker.

No matter what precautions a security team takes, no network is ever going to be 100% secure. Security professionals used to joke that the only way to protect a network is to disconnect it from the Internet and shut down all of the computers. Today's skilled attackers have methods for exfiltrating data from a closed network, and even a turned off computer can leak information.

To move to an Intelligence-Guided Computer Network Defense (IGCND) model a security organization must first change their thinking regarding network security. An IGCND model will help organizations significantly improve their effectiveness in stopping attacks, but it will not stop all attacks. The real benefit of the intelligence-led security is that it helps organizations adapt quickly to those attacks that were missed and put in protections that will prevent the attacks from recurring. The other benefit of intelligence-led security is that it affords security team the ability to be more proactive in their security posture. Understanding the coming threats allows security teams to put protections in place days or weeks before the actual attack happens. This second aspect changes the metrics the security teams deliver to management from "we cleaned 50 infected laptops last month" to "we saved the company $750,000 by preventing those laptops from getting infected in the first place."

IGCND is about gaining a full understanding of the organization, including the business side of the organization, and building protection strategies around the keeping the things that are most valuable to the organization safe.

This chapter discusses two different security frameworks: the Continuous Monitoring framework and the Cybersecurity Framework. These are just two of the many different cyber security frameworks that are out there. Finding a framework that is a good fit for an organization is critical to the success of moving the organization from being event-driven to intelligence-led.

THE CONTINUOUS MONITORING FRAMEWORK

Keeping the network safe starts with understanding what is on the network. One of the best regarded frameworks for doing this is the Continuous Monitoring Framework. The National Institute of Standards and Technology (NIST) first introduced the idea of Continuous Monitoring in 2010 in NIST Special Publication 800-37: *Guide for Applying the Risk Management Framework to Federal Information Systems*. Continuous Monitoring for information technology systems was further refined in NIST Special Publication 800-137: *Information Security Continuous Monitoring (ISCM) for Federal Information Systems and Organizations*. NIST Special Publications 800-137 defines continuous monitoring as:

> *Information security continuous monitoring (ISCM) is defined as maintaining on-going awareness of information security, vulnerabilities, and threats to support organizational risk management decisions (NIST, 2011, p. vi).*

The definition is simple, but the implementation is complex. Continuous monitoring helps organizations improve situational awareness by maintaining a constant understanding of the status of the network and the threats against the network. By collecting information around the security posture of the network, internal data, and combining that with an understanding of the current threat level, external data, a security team has the best chance of stopping threats.

Continuous monitoring is an active security strategy. Staying ahead of threats against the network means not waiting until there is a network infection before taking preventative steps. It also means adapting to changes in the threat environment, as the threats change the security precautions in the network must also change. Finally, continuous monitoring means continually communicating the state of security with the appropriate stakeholders, making sure everyone is briefed who needs to be at an appropriate time and appropriate level.

Similar to the intelligence cycle described in Chapter 2 (see p. 0000), under NIST the continuous monitoring framework is a circular model consisting of six parts: Define, Establish, Implement, Analyze and Report, Respond, and Review and Update.

To define a continuous monitoring strategy within an organization means having a complete view of network assets, understanding the vulnerabilities within those assets, and keeping up-to-date on the latest threats against those assets. Defining a strategy also means understanding the bigger picture, which includes not only understanding what data is critical to the organization, it also means understanding the impact to the organization if that data is lost or stolen. Finally, it means understanding the risk profile of the organization. While the security team may have one level of risk profile, leadership within the organization may have a different profile. Knowing this information and building a continuous monitoring strategy around it is critical to the success of a security organization.

The next step in the continuous monitoring process is to establish a program with clearly defined and measurable metrics. This phase also includes information about monitoring frequencies and security assessments as well as a technical overview of how the continuous monitoring program will work.

Implementation is the phase where everything comes together and is actually put into place. During the implementation phase everything comes together and is put into action. Putting everything on paper is one thing, but going through the process of implementation can pose unexpected challenges. Management buy-in is very important in this stage, to help overcome any unexpected obstacles.

Once the process has been implemented, the next step is to analyze the results of the implementation to ensure that the data being collected is what was originally expected. Once the data is analyzed, security teams should report on the findings, to make sure they are providing the necessary information. Anything that is not meeting expectations should be adjusted until it meets the expected metrics, or the metrics should be changed to meet the data collected.

Analyzing and reporting on security incidents is not enough. For a security program to be effective, the security team must respond to events that originate during the analyze-and-report phase. After a major breach, how many times has a story come out that security control "X" caught the intruder, but the alert was ignored? The answer to that is too many. No matter how good a security program is or how many security tools are in place, if alerts are ignored, for whatever reason, they are not operating effectively.

Which is where the last phase of the continuous monitoring framework comes into play. A continuous monitoring program must be constantly reviewed and updated. Just as the intelligence cycle is a continuous process, so is continuous monitoring. If alerts are missed, there should be a review as to why, and determine how they might not be missed in the future. A common problem security teams report is that a particular vendor provides too many false-positives, so they ignore it. If a product is providing too many false-positives in this model, it should be removed from the network and replaced with a more effective tool. Alternatively, data from that vendor should be better correlated against other data to automatically lower the severity of the false-positives while still processing real alerts at the correct warning level.

Because of its roots in NIST, continuous monitoring is often associated with government agencies, but the principals behind continuous monitoring are applicable to any organization that is looking to improve its security posture and gain better situational awareness.

NIST CYBERSECURITY FRAMEWORK

Version 1.0 of the NIST Cybersecurity framework was published in February 2014, but the genesis of its development was President Obama's Executive Order 13636, which was released on February 12, 2013 and entitled "Improving Critical Infrastructure Cybersecurity." The stated goal of the Cybersecurity Framework is that it "…calls for the development of a voluntary risk-based Cybersecurity Framework – a set of industry standards and best practices to help organizations manage cybersecurity risk" (NIST, 2014a).

Like continuous monitoring the Cybersecurity Framework is not platform specific, nor does it create a new regulatory infrastructure with which organizations have to comply. Instead, the framework allows organizations to improve their security using existing platforms and regulations, improving security processes rather than adding additional hardware/software or regulatory guidelines.

The Cybersecurity Framework is broken into three parts: The Framework Core, Framework Implementation Tiers, and Framework Profile. The three parts work together to help create a security plan that assesses the current state of the security program and builds a stronger program over time.

THE FRAMEWORK CORE

The Framework Core is a matrix that identifies the actions that need to be taken within a tier to successfully meet the cyber security outcomes of that tier. The Framework Core for a tier 1 organization looks very different than that of a tier 2 organization, but both operate within the same framework.

The Framework Core matrix, in its simplest form, is a table that uses four elements to document progress towards meeting security goals, along with the standards on which those goals are based. The four elements that make up the Framework Core are Functions, Categories, Subcategories, and Informative References. The structure

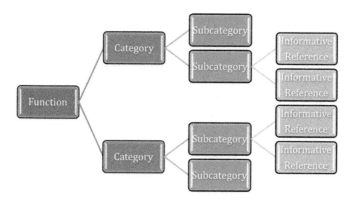

FIGURE 4.1

Framework core workflow.

is similar to the flowchart outline in Figure 4.1. Functions are fixed elements in the table, but everything else is variable based on the sector, maturity level, and security information specific to the organization.

Within the Framework Core there are five different security functions defined. Those five functions are: Identify, Protect, Detect, Respond, and Recover. These five functions map to security areas within the organization. Categories break down the functions into security programs within the organization such as Vulnerability Management or Log Collection. Subcategories further break down categories into day-to-day activities carried out by the security team that enable fulfillment of the larger categories. For example, weekly "vulnerability scanning" would be a subcategory of the larger category of Vulnerability Management, and "configure VPN concentrators to send logs to ArcSight" would be a subcategory of "Log Collection."

Informative references are industry standards that apply to each subcategory and serve as useful guidelines to achieving the stated outcome in the subcategory. These standards can be broad, like Payment Card Industry Data Security Standard (PCI DSS) or Federal Information Security Management Act (FISMA), or they can be very specific such as NIST Special Publication 800-123, which deals with server security. Informative references can be used as a guideline to implementation of the security categories, but they should not be the only guideline. Organizations often security have needs above and beyond industry standards. The focus should be on the security needs of the organization rather than meeting an arbitrary standard (unless those standards are legal requirements that the organization is audited against).

Identify, Protect, Detect, Respond, and Recover are the five functions that align with various roles within the security organization (though a security analyst usually plays more than one role within an organization). Activities under the Identify function are those responsible for gaining a better insight into the network and organization, a better situational awareness based on better understanding of "systems, assets, data and capabilities" (NIST, 2014b). This function involves categories like

Asset Management, Business Intelligence, Risk Assessment, and Risk Management Strategies.

Protect is the function that security teams are most familiar with, this is the ability of an organization to protect the assets identified as part of the Identity function. Again, the Cybersecurity Framework assumes organization have been, or will be successfully breached, how well are the critical assets of an organization protected? This function covers categories like Security Training, Access Control, Information Protection Controls and Data Security.

The Detect function is all about the ability of the security team to discover malicious activity as quickly as possible. This is really a test of how well the Protect function is implemented, not that a well-protected network should never be breached, but that the intruder should be quickly detected. Categories in this function include Anomaly Detection, Event Monitoring, and Continuous Monitoring.

The Respond function is about the ability of an organization to react to a detected security event and take appropriate and quick action to contain the event. Again, the Respond function does not work unless proper detection mechanisms are in place and being monitored. Respond categories include Planning, Event Analysis, Communications, and Mitigation Strategies.

The final function, Recover, is the ability of an organization to return to normal following a breach. How quickly can systems be restored? How fast can normal operations resume with high confidence that the threat is removed and new protections are in place? Categories that are part of this function include Communications, Incident Recovery, and Improvements.

Although each of these functions builds on the others, they do not have to be implemented sequentially. In fact, sequential implementation would be a poor security strategy. Instead, they should be implemented simultaneously. Most organizations already have some or all of the these functions partially implemented, so adding to existing capabilities while implementing new functions, should be part of the Cybersecurity Framework planning.

FRAMEWORK IMPLEMENTATION TIERS

The framework provides for four tiers that reflect the level of security maturity of the organization. The four tiers are: Partial, Risk Informed, Repeatable, and Adaptive. Each tier is a reflection of how the organization views security risks and the level of preparedness to deal with these risks.

Determining the current tier level requires examining an organization's current risk management practices as well as the threats against the organization and regulatory requirements. Each of these aspects of a security programs needs to be contrasted against the objectives of the organization as well as any organizational limitations. Essentially, to determine in which tier an organization resides it must take a frank look at its current security stance and determine how much willingness there is within the organization to change. There are some areas that will be outside the control of an organization. For example, regulatory requirements may force an organization to be at a higher tier level than they want to be, at least for some categories. Similarly, an organization has no control over the threats to their organization. When source code for a point of sale (POS) malware kit was publicly released in 2013, it suddenly made the barrier of entry to collecting credit card data from compromised retail organizations a lot lower; that is, a change to the threat environment over which those organizations had no control. Organizations with POS systems in place did have control over whether or not they were going to adjust their risk management practices in light of this new development – many chose not to and paid a price in loss of customer trust.

Each tier in the Cybersecurity Framework is divided into three parts: Risk Management Process, Integrated Risk Management Program, and External Participations. Each tier reflects a different maturity level and therefore a different capability for each part of the tier.

At tier 1, Partial, an organization has a very informal Risk Management Process. These organizations are the epitome of "Whack-a-Mole" security, there is no cohesive security plan and security investments are not tied to organizational needs. Unsurprisingly, these organizations also have very unsophisticated Integrated Risk Management Program with very little information about the cyber security program being shared with management. Generally, security information in tier 1 organizations is not shared within the organization or with other organizations that could benefit from the information, which means there is little to no External Participation.

Tier 2 organizations are Risk Informed. Being Risk Informed means that an organization has management buy-in and approval for its Risk Management Process. This process is directly informed by the organizational objectives. While the Risk Management Process has been formalized within the organization, the Integrated Risk Management Program is less formalized. Although leadership is aware of and participating in the risk management program, there is limited participation by the rest of the organization, outside of the security team. Training and communication within the organization is still ad-hoc, but it is being conducted. Finally, while the organization is more aware of its role within the larger security community it does not have processes in place that allow it to share in External Participation.

Tier 3, Repeatable, is a more mature security organization. The Risk Management Process not only includes involvement by organizational leadership, it is also expressed as a policy that is communicated to the organization. The Risk Management Process is informed and updated by changes in the threat landscape as well as objectives changes within the organization. There is also an organizational-wide approach to the Integrated Risk Management Program. Not only are cyber security policies implemented with respect to the organization's cyber risk needs, they are also communicated to the entire organization. There are checks in place to ensure that the policies and procedures are being carried out correctly and meeting the desired outcome. The organization is more involved in External Participation. It understands who its partners are, and where it fits into the larger cyber security picture. It receives regular information from partners that informs cyber security decisions internally.

Tier 4 is Adaptive; it is the most advanced level in the Cybersecurity Framework. The Risk Management Process in tier 4 is much more predictive, rather than reactive. The entire organization adapts to changes in the security environment, not just the leadership and the security team. The Integrated Risk Management Program in this tier is part of the organizational culture. Everyone is aware of the risks and security policies are understood and communicated on a regular basis. The organization operates in a continuous monitoring mode; always evolving based on previous incidents and expected malicious activity that will target the organization. In tier 4 External Participation is more than simply receiving and processing security information from peers. Instead the organization shares information with other organization and takes more of a leadership role in its sector, leading other organizations in the sector to better security practices and improving security for everyone.

Although it is possible for organizations to be at different tiers for different aspects of the security process, that is generally not the case. After all, if a security team has trouble getting leadership buy-in to the security program, it is doubtful that the organization is an active member of the sector's Information Sharing and Analysis Center (ISAC). Jumping from one tier to the next is not necessarily the purpose of the Cybersecurity Framework. Even though continuous organizational improvement within the security team is always important, sometimes jumping from one tier to the next does not make organizational sense. As the Cybersecurity Framework states, "Progression to higher Tiers is encouraged when such a change would reduce cybersecurity risk and be cost effective" (NIST, 2014c). As with continuous monitoring, the point of the Cybersecurity Framework is not to find new ways to help organizations spend money; instead, the point is how to make the best use of the systems that are in place and formalize the policies and processes so that they are repeatable across the organization.

THE FRAMEWORK PROFILE

The Framework Profile in the intersection of the Framework Core with the Framework Implementation Tiers. The Framework Profile takes the information collected about the Functions, Categories and Subcategories and the information collected from the Risk Management Process, Integrated Risk Management Profile, and External Participation reviews to build an understanding of where the organization is on the Cybersecurity Framework. A Framework Profile does not have to be all-encompassing – different parts of the organization can have different Framework Profiles, depending on their level of maturity and their security needs.

As has been emphasized throughout this section, the Framework Profile must align with the organization's goals, strategies, and business direction. It is not enough to simply have requirements based on security needs; it is just as important to understand the larger business/organizational requirements and build the Framework Profile with an understanding of and nod to both sets of requirements.

Most organizations have two Framework Profiles, the first is the current Framework Profile and the second is the aspirational profile. The current Framework Profile is an honest look at the current state of security within the organization and honest look at the organization's abilities against the Framework Core and the Implementation Tiers. The aspirational Framework Profile should be the desired state of the security team within the organization.

It is important not to take the notion of "aspirational" too literally when building out the two Framework Profiles. The aspirational Framework Profile should still be attainable given the realities of the organization, that means having an honest discussion between organizational leadership and the security team. For example, the organization may be many years away from being at a Tier 4 Implementation Tier, or may never reach that level. In that case, the organization should not set its aspirational Framework Profile to Adaptive. Many organizations are able to reach the Risk Informed tier, and if that is the case, that should be set as the target Framework Profile.

Once the current and target Framework Profiles have been identified, to include the steps necessary to achieve success at both profiles, the next step is to identify what the gaps are between the current and target Framework Profiles. Once the gaps are identified, the security team can work with leadership to build an action plan to address those gaps and move the organization to the target tier.

Gaps should be prioritized based on the needs of the organization, whether those needs are business driven or driven by risk mitigation (hopefully, as an organization matures along these tiers, those two drivers will become more intertwined). Once the gaps are identified an action plan needs to be developed, with buy-in from organizational leadership and the security team, to address the gaps in a timely manner.

The Cybersecurity Framework can seem complicated at first. Many security leaders are not used to thinking in business terms. Overwhelmed security teams may be used to seeing organizational leadership as an obstacle to better security, rather than a partner. However, by taking the time to change the security conversation so it is more reflective of the business goals and objectives of the larger organization, getting leadership support becomes easier. Having the support of the organizational leadership also means that the security team will be more effective at getting the security plan implemented and be more successful at protecting the organization.

SECURITY + INTELLIGENCE

Both of these frameworks are a good start in terms of creating situational awareness, but neither takes into account intelligence sources that can help improve security. In fact, throughout NIST Special Publication 800-137, the word intelligence is only used twice, both times to describe the definition of a National Security System. In the NIST Cybersecurity Framework intelligence is not mentioned at all.

On the other hand, the SANS Institute offers an interesting take on continuous monitoring, with their white paper entitled, "A Real-Time Approach to Continuous Monitoring" (Tarala, 2011).

In the paper, author James Tarala (2011) breaks continuous monitoring down into four components:

- Vulnerability and Asset Management
- System and log collection, correlation and reporting
- Advanced network monitoring
- Threat intelligence and business analytics.

These components of continuous monitoring are useful because they create clearly defined boundaries that allow for a phased approach to continuous monitoring. So, an organization with a security team that is drowning in alerts with no clear path to better security now has a place to start.

This list of components is also useful because it includes an intelligence overlay. It also goes a step further than most models because it includes both threat intelligence and business intelligence as part of its core components. Too often, when security teams think of intelligence, they only think about cyber threat intelligence, but the business component is an important aspect.

By following the steps outlined in the SANS approach to continuous monitoring an organization is able to easily move through three phases to becoming a fully intelligence-led security organization. That doesn't mean that a security team needs to sit down and plan the first phase then get around to the second phase when time permits (let's be honest, there will never be time). Instead, the plan needs to be in place from the start, following the guidelines outlined in NIST Special Publication 800-37 (or whatever the chosen model is), and implemented along a predefined timeline. Continuous monitoring, with an intelligence overlay, needs to become ingrained in the daily habits of everyone involved in security within an organization.

Many organizations are already at least partially implementing each of the three phases outlined, but not necessarily in a cohesive manner. In fact, as has already been mentioned a number of times, many organizations are implementing their security systems with no thought as to the interconnection to other systems. Even beyond that, the security team often does not have insight into tools that would enable them to improve situational awareness.

Vulnerability scanning is a perfect example of this phenomenon. The security team needs to know what systems exist on the network, what functions they serve, and how they are configured. If that information is stored at all, it is most often stored in a Governance, Risk Management, and Compliance (GRC) solution. That GRC solution is managed by the team responsible for compliance within the organization – the team that works with auditors and is responsible for staying compliant with any industry-specific regulations to which the organization must adhere. But, if the security team learns of an immediate threat, involving a new vulnerability in a platform in use on the network, they do not have the visibility into the network to see what the organizational risk is.

In a continuous monitoring framework, doing enough work to meet regulatory compliance is not the goal. Instead, the goal is to provide an active defense against the threats targeting the network. Which means, ultimately, being able to process internal and external changes to the threat landscape in real time and being able to report and act on those changes in a timely manner.

Forget the scenario outlined above where the security team doesn't have visibility into the assets on the network. Instead, imagine an organization where the security team stops a new piece of malware at the edge of the network. The security team has that malware analyzed and receives a report on the exploits being used. The security team is able to instantly identify the vulnerabilities associated with those exploits and is able to pull together a list of systems that are vulnerable. Based on the severity of the exploit and the number of systems in the network that are vulnerable to it, it is able to assign a risk rating specific to the network. Separately, based on the malware analysis, the security team is able to identify the adversary behind the attack and what other organizations that adversary is targeting. Within a few hours – a day at most – the security team is able to brief management about the nature of the threat and provide a comprehensive overview of the threat posed to the network and the precautions taken to mitigate that threat.

For many organizations, the previous paragraph may has well have been written by Philip K. Dick, as it represents more science fiction than any relationship to reality. If it can be done, it will cost more than the entire IT budget, much less the paltry budget most security teams have available with which to work.

The truth is, most organizations have the capability today to implement a security monitoring strategy. Almost every organization has a GRC tool (sometimes more than one), just as almost every organization has security protection at the edge and on the desktop. There are even a large number of organizations that have invested in Security Information and Event Management (SIEM) and network monitoring solutions. The problem is not that systems needed for continuous monitoring are not in the networks; the problem is that they are not talking to each other.

The security industry is not entirely without blame here. Customers of security vendors have been asking, begging, cajoling, and demanding for years that security vendors should make it easy for products of one vendor to communicate with products from other vendors. In many cases, two products from the same vendor cannot even easily speak to each other. If a security company cannot get its own products to talk to each other, how are they going to get their product to communicate with another vendor's product? Fortunately, this mindset is rapidly changing in the world of security. Gone are the days when a security company assumed an organization would use its products exclusively. The trend today is toward networks that contain multiple security products from multiple vendors and security vendors who are more responsive to their customer needs and are more willing to build connectors to third party products at their customer request.

Conversely, more vendors are opening their platforms and publishing standards that allow other vendors to connect to them. Some of the larger security companies are still slow to adapt to this intercommunication, and that is reflected by their loss of market share to younger, nimbler companies that will provide customers with the connections to other platforms that they need.

That is how most security teams wound up drowning in alerts, every time a new security problem was introduced vendors recommended a new product to solve the problem. The term *agent fatigue* is widely used to describe this phenomenon on the desktop. Are viruses a problem? Here is an antivirus solution. Is command and control communication the problem? Here is a Host-based Intrusion Detection System (HIDS). Need to keep track of all the software and versions installed on a system? Here is a compliance agent. The list of agents goes on and on. Each agent serves a different purpose, communicates to a different control server, and is managed by a different group within the organization.

Working within a security framework and building a security plan is not about purchasing a lot of new technology. Instead, the goal with a security plan is to take advantage of the technology that exists in the network and make it work better. Think about the number of security technologies in a typical network, the overlap in capabilities of some of those technologies, and the number of unused features. There are undoubtedly security products in most networks that are not being used to their full potential. Either because the security team does not know about the new capabilities, or it is slated to be tested at some point, but the security team has not had time to get to it yet.

A good security plan takes all of this into account. It addresses the reality of the lack of time every security team faces and determines what needs to be done to overcome those problems and move forward to better security with improved situational awareness.

THE BUSINESS SIDE OF SECURITY

Building an intelligence-led security strategy, whether using a continuous monitoring framework, Cybersecurity Framework, or another security, requires being able to translate security activities into a language that the business side of the organization can understand.

Security teams, and even chief information security officers (CISOs), tend to speak in technical terms. Security leaders say things like, "We blocked 3000 attacking IP addresses last month" or "We stopped 20% more spam." These are important, but they don't make a business case for why security is so important to the organization. Of course, the security industry doesn't help as these are the same types of metrics that security vendors use to sell their products. Security vendors will tell their customers things like, "We release 100,000 new signatures a month" or "Our product is capable of monitoring at 1000 Gbps."

None of these conversations translate into something that explains to the business side of the organization what value the security spend adds to the bottom line. But it doesn't have to be that way. The evidence for the return on investment that good security practices deliver to organizations appears every day on news sites and the nightly news. The costs associated with a major breach are well documented and demonstrated every time a large company or government organization discloses a missed attack.

According to the Ponemon Institute report, "2014 Cost of Data Breach Study" the average cost of a data breach to an organization is $3.5 million (Ponemon Institute, 2014).

Building an intelligence-led security program allows the security team to change the conversation from one involving bits and bytes to one involving cost savings and value demonstration. It also allows the security team to focus on the larger picture when presenting to senior management or the board.

How does that work? It starts by switching away from discussions about irrelevant numbers. Every organization of any size it targeted by hundreds or thousands of security attacks each day. Trying to turn hundreds or thousands of security incidents each day into increased budget numbers won't work, as evidenced by the fact that security budgets continue to shrink despite the fact that the number of attacks against any organization are on the rise. Instead of discussing the number of attacks, the focus should be on those attacks that most relevant to the organization, and could have caused the most damage to the organization's reputation.

The only way to understand which attacks could have caused the most damage to the organization is through the use of cyber threat intelligence. At its most effective, cyber threat intelligences allows an organization to connect artifacts to tools and to adversaries. By tying indicators of compromise to the adversaries behind those indicators, security teams are able to not only focus efforts on those threats that pose the greatest risk to the organization, but explain those actions in terms of tangible savings to the organization.

For example, there are thousands of new vulnerabilities discovered each day. An organization that is able to automate the prioritization of patching vulnerable systems using the Common Vulnerability Scoring System (CVSS) presents a tangible value in terms of manpower saved. Taking it to the next level and prioritizing based not only on the CVSS score, but also on intelligence, such as whether or not the vulnerability is being exploited in the wild and what groups are behind the exploitation, changes the conversation again. Now the conversation is not one of just man-hours; now it is a conversation built around the damage the adversary using an exploit targeting a vulnerability that exists within the organization can cause, based on what that adversary has done in the past. An adversary who has a track record of gaining access to networks and exfiltrating valuable data poses a more significant risk, and an increased cost to the organization if successful, than just a known vulnerability with no context.

The business conversation does not just revolve around threats; it also revolves around justifying the addition of new staff or technology. Instead of discussing the need to increase budget to add a security widget, the conversation changes to adding capability in order to achieve success in meeting the next goal in the IGCND model. Remember that whatever framework is being used to move toward intelligence-led security requires the buy-in from senior management. By expressing new requests in terms of filling gaps in the next phase of the plan, security teams are simply helping to meet the agreed upon goals set by the organization.

From this perspective, adding a new incident response tool does not mean that the security team will be able to respond to security incidents 20% faster. Instead, it means that it fills a gap in phase four of the security plan, which requires proactive protections be in place to prevent security events before they become a problem.

One thing to keep in mind when trying to discuss security in business terms: senior management and the board read the same news stories as the security team. Most board members are aware, albeit sometimes vaguely, of the threats facing their organization. They see the competitors in the news because of the breach that wound up leaking a million credit cards, and they don't want to be next. The leadership of the organization has an obligation to protect the organization and its assets from outside threats. The leadership wants to enable the security team to protect the organization and, as long as the requests are put in a language that leadership speaks, they will do so.

PLANNING A PHASED APPROACH

Whether an organization opts for a continuous monitoring framework, the Cybersecurity Framework, or one of the many other security frameworks, a phased approach to meeting the security goals of the organization is highly recommended. A phased approach allows an organization to take stock of the current status of the organization's security program and decide where the organization should be. Moving from the current state to the desired state requires an action plan and a timeline for implementation. Pulling all of this together in a way that can be easily understood by all involved and that metrics can be set against is challenging, but in the end will result in better protection for the organization and its assets.

THE GOAL

Before colleting any data, the first step is for the security team to sit down with organizational leadership and define an end goal. The goal of almost any security framework is to move the organization toward the point of near real-time identification of and response to security incidents, as well as improved situational awareness of the threats posed to the organization. There are other side effects of the security improvement process that can become stated goals such as improved employee security awareness, better compliance reporting and improved communication with the leadership of the organization. Alternatively, if an organization is early in the security maturity process the primary goal of the initial phase may be better compliance reporting, and everything else becomes a phase two and beyond goal.

Whatever, the initial goals are, they need to be well documented and have management support. The goals also need to be communicated to the relevant stakeholder within the organization. Anyone who is going to be impacted by the change in the security program (or in some cases by the creation of a security program) should be notified and informed of their role in the process so they have time to prepare.

THE INITIAL ASSESSMENT

Many organizations don't like to hear this, but it is usually a good idea to involve a third party in the initial assessment, assuming that third party is used correctly. The truth is, many organizations do not know what their security gaps are or whether those gaps are organizational or technology based. Having a security expert assist with the initial assessment can be invaluable in terms of getting started on the right track toward building an intelligence-led security program.

Another key consideration during the initial assessment is bringing in trusted technology and security vendors that already support the organization. Yes, these vendors have a vested interest in keeping their products around, but they have great insight into what similar organizations are doing to confront the same security challenges. That is an important point to remember: No matter how unique an organization is, there are other organizations who have faced similar, if not the exact same, security challenges.

Consider, for example, companies that might exist in multiple sectors. A company may be a manufacturer, a member of the critical infrastructure and may even have a financial services arm. It also may be big enough that its adversaries develop special tools and use unique infrastructure just to target it. That doesn't necessarily make the cyber threat to its organization unique. It may be unique in that it has to ward off multiple types of threats, but those threats are being used against other companies in that sector. Even if a threat is unique targeted toward that organization, the adversary behind the threat has undoubtedly used the same tactics, techniques, and procedures (TTPs) against other organizations. The company can learn from other attacks made by that adversary and improve the security of the organizations.

This is one of the biggest complaints that security professionals have about the term *advanced persistent threat* (APT). APT is used as a buzzword by a lot of security vendors to describe a long-term, targeted attack. Calling these attacks APTs implies that there is something special about the attack. The truth is, proper security processes and procedures with the right detection methods being continuously monitored will identify almost all so-called APT attacks.

In addition to outside consultants and technology vendors, the initial conversation should also involve the organization's auditors. A big part of the initial assessment is gaining an understanding of both the security state and the regulatory state. Knowing what standards the organization must follow to remain in compliance with government and industry standards is as important as understanding network traffic flows within the organization.

Other groups within the organization must be involved as well. If servers, databases, desktops, routers, VPNs are managed by groups outside of security they should be involved in the conversation. Any cloud-based applications should be understood and the people who manage those applications should be included in the conversation. Human resources need to be involved in the initial assessment as they often serve as the conduit to the rest of the organization. Finally, the people in the organization who maintain the most valuable assets need to be involved in the initial assessment.

Does everyone need to be involved at the same time by setting up a giant meeting at the local stadium? No. In fact, for the initial assessment, the security team should meet with each group individually to conduct interviews. The goal is to understand the security processes and procedures as they exist today. This allows the security team to get a feel for the "day in the life" of each person within the organization and gain a better understanding of the reality of the organization's security profile from those outside the organization.

One group not mentioned so far in this conversation is the leadership of the organization. The first meeting in planning the migration from "Whack-a-Mole" security to being intelligence driven should be with the leadership of the organization. Once the leadership understands the benefits and buys into the concept, everything else is easier – note, not easy, just easier.

The goal of the initial assessment is to understand the where the organization is today in terms of security, and that should be its only goal. Too many security teams get caught up in trying to immediately identify gaps during the assessment phase, which is a big mistake. Until the target state is identified and signed off on by all stakeholders, identifying gaps is just falling back into the trap of ad-hoc security.

ANALYZING THE CURRENT SECURITY STATE

Once the relevant stakeholders have been interviewed and the necessary information has been gathered, the next step is to identify the current state of security across the organization and place that state into the chosen security framework. Again, organizational leadership needs to be heavily involved in this step. All stakeholders will need to agree on analysis of the current state, especially those stakeholders who appear less effective, security-wise, than their peers. Often, this is where an outside security consultant can be important; the consultant can act as a neutral third party. Plotting the current security state is not meant to be an adversarial exercise with other groups within the organization, but it can seem that way. Reassuring everyone involved in advance, and throughout the process, that the sole purpose of the exercise is to improve the security of organization can help smooth the process (though, not always).

The chosen framework is not important as long it is enough to take into account all of the security variables within the organization. It should not be too technology or compliance focused; instead, it should take into account both sides of the security coin. This is one of the reasons that the NIST Cybersecurity Framework has garnered so much support. The Cybersecurity Framework provides organizations with the ability to take an expansive look at all aspects of their security program.

For the purposes of this book, the SANS Continuous Monitoring model written by Tarala (2011) will do. It works for three reasons:

- It offers a multiphased approach to building a security program.
- It breaks technologies down into natural groups.
- It is extensible, giving organizations the ability to add compliance and intelligence needs.

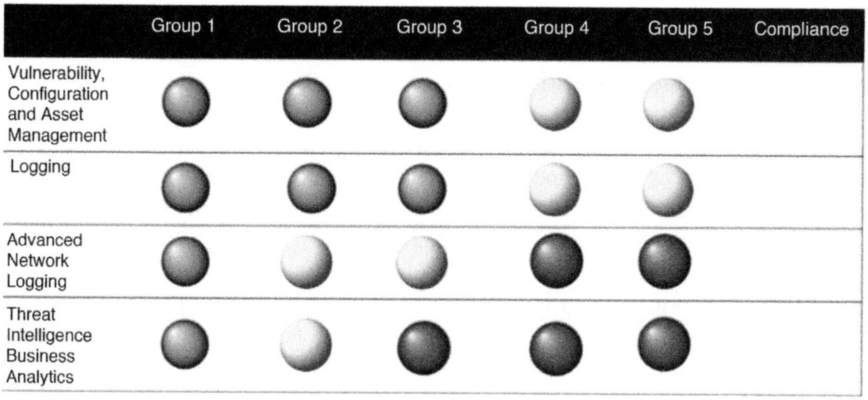

	Group 1	Group 2	Group 3	Group 4	Group 5	Compliance
Vulnerability, Configuration and Asset Management	●	●	●	○	○	
Logging	●	●	●	○	○	
Advanced Network Logging	●	○	○	●	●	
Threat Intelligence Business Analytics	●	○	●	●	●	

FIGURE 4.2

Phase one continuous monitoring dashboard.

There are some limitations to this framework that may not make it suitable for all organizations, but it is a good start.

One positive about the SANS model is that in addition to creating natural groupings of technologies based on the way most organizations use those technologies, it also groups by centralized collection points. This makes documenting the current state of security relatively easy, using a chart similar to that in Figure 4.2.

Within the SANS framework each group in the organization is responsible. Phase one of the SANS model, generally involves ad-hoc collections processes, but assumes all of the data is available to be queried as needed.

Keeping that in mind, using a chart similar to that shown in Figure 4.2, the security team can quickly map which groups within the organization are meeting the stated requirements for phase one and which areas need focus. The chart also leaves room to discuss compliance needs for each of the requirements section, and, of course, can be adjusted to account for other factors, or break down the components into subcomponents to track progress at a more granular level. Another option is to document the progress in the chart directly, rather than creating a simple dashboard. Again, the beauty of using an open framework is that it is customizable to the needs of the organization.

Of course, just having the dashboard is not enough. There should be supporting documentation for each of the groups and each of the components, based on the initial investigative work that was done. The team managing the security program build-out should be able to get current status of the progress at a glance.

MOVING TO THE NEXT PHASE

When moving toward an IGCND model, just as with any security framework, the security team should have outlined the current security state as well as the target security state. In the previous section, the process for collecting information and building a baseline was outlined. Concurrent with that effort should be planning where the organization wants to go.

Underpinning the chart in Figure 4.2 is a set of requirements that are part of the baseline signed-off on by the organizational leadership in the first phase. A baseline set of requirement for the second phase should also be outlined and then mapped out in a chart similar to the one used for the first phase. So, while the fields remain the same, the requirements for success are different.

For example, to meet the requirements for logging in phase one of the plan, a group within the organization may simply have to keep logs locally on all systems for at least 90 days. For phase two, those logs have to be kept for 90 days and must also be sent to a centralized collection point, such as SIEM.

Once the monitoring evolves from decentralized and ad-hoc to centralized and processed it becomes easier to inject intelligence into the process. Simply put, the data collected from the components in the continuous monitoring process become raw data that the security team can analyze and build intelligence alerts around. Continuous monitoring improves the ability of an organization to apply that intelligence overlay to the security processes. But, an organization must walk before it can run. So, starting out by understanding what the current state of security is within the organization, then moving toward a centralized collection model for relevant security data, and finally combining collected data with intelligence allows an organization to create a truly intelligence-led security program.

CONCLUSION

For a security program to be effective, it must operate inside an agreed upon framework. That framework should include standard definitions and requirements for each phase of the security process. Once the framework has been created, and signed off on by organizational leadership, it should be shared with the relevant stakeholders within the rest of the organization. Having leadership support throughout the process is critical as that helps unify the entire organization behind the security process.

Once the framework has been developed, it is important to interview the relevant stakeholders, both inside and outside the organization, to truly understand the nature of the systems and processes they support.

Using the framework and the information gathered during the interview process an organization can build a security baseline that reflect the current state of the program. Once the baseline has been captured, the next step is to understand where the gaps are and create an action place that allows all groups within the organization to meet the baseline requirements.

When the baseline requirements are met across the organization, the next step is to create an action plan that move the entire organization to the next phase. Each phase in the security process should maintain the same components, but with different goals for each of those components.

This process is not always any easy one, but if it is laid out correctly and has leadership backing and the support of the organization then it can be successful. As Sun Tzu said, "He will win whose army is animated by the same spirit throughout all its ranks."

REFERENCES

National Institute of Standards and Technology (NIST), 2014a. Framework for improving critical infrastructure cybersecurity version 1. <http://www.nist.gov/cyberframework/upload/cybersecurity-framework-021214.pdf> (accessed 23.08.14.), p. 1.

National Institute of Standards and Technology (NIST), 2014b. Framework for improving critical infrastructure cybersecurity version 1. <http://www.nist.gov/cyberframework/upload/cybersecurity-framework-021214.pdf> (accessed 23.08.14.), p. 8.

National Institute of Standards and Technology (NIST), 2014c. Framework for improving critical infrastructure cybersecurity version 1. <http://www.nist.gov/cyberframework/upload/cybersecurity-framework-021214.pdf> (accessed 23.08.14.), p. 9.

Ponemon Institute, 2014. 2014 Cost of data breach study. <http://www-935.ibm.com/services/us/en/it-services/security-services/cost-of-data-breach/> (accessed 23.08.14.).

Tarala, J., 2011. A real-time approach to continuous monitoring. <http://www.sans.org/reading-room/whitepapers/analyst/real-time-approach-continuous-monitoring-34950>. (accessed 23.08.14.).

Internal intelligence sources

INFORMATION IN THIS CHAPTER:

- Asset, Vulnerability, and Configuration Management
- Network Logging
- Network Monitoring

INTRODUCTION

Planning is now complete. Now it is time to start collecting the data that will eventually become the intelligence that improves the security of the network. There are two schools of thought on what should be collected from the network. The first is to collect everything that can be collected. There is some logic to this school. After all, attackers are getting better at what they do and are always finding new and creative ways to infiltrate networks. The last thing a security team wants to find out is that they missed an attack because they were not monitoring data on a specific device.

The second school of thought says that logs should only be collected from devices that can provide anomalous data alerts or provide an indicator that the security team can pivot off of to match against other sources. This also makes sense. Data that is being collected but not monitored in an automated fashion by the security team is effectively useless in a cyber security environment, especially in a cyber security environment that is moving from reactive to proactive.

A compromise that works for many organizations is to gradually collect more complex data as the organization progresses through the tiers from reactive to proactive and intelligence-driven security. During the early phases it is important to catalogue all data and have an awareness of how to access it should the need arise, but actual collection and processing of complex data sources can wait until later phases.

ASSET, VULNERABILITY, AND CONFIGURATION MANAGEMENT

Sun Tzu said, "If you know the enemy and know yourself, you need not fear the result of a hundred battles." Of course, Sun Tzu never envisioned a time when security teams would engage in a hundred battles or more every day.

While the scope may be different, the basic idea remains the same almost 2500 years later. To protect the network and effectively defend against attackers, a security team must be able to look into every aspect of the organization. The team has to know what systems exist on the network, what people are using the network, and what is the expected behavior of both the people and the assets.

A good place to start is with asset management. In its most basic form asset management involves an accounting of all the systems that are on the network. A simple scan of each of the organization's networks, from inside those networks, will provide a very basic asset map. But generally that is not enough. Using an asset discovery tool such as Nessus (www.tenable.com) or Qualys (www.qualys.com) will not only allow a security team to find systems on the network, it will also help identify what type of systems they are and what ports are open on the systems.

Of course, these asset-discovery systems should be used in conjunction with working with different groups in the organization to find out for which systems each group is responsible. Too often in the realm of network security, the focus is on the technology or tools that can be used to solve a problem, rather than the people that can be used to solve the same problem.

Asset discovery tools are extremely valuable, but so is having a conversation with the team responsible for the systems being discovered. Collecting the information up front, through the interview process, makes the asset discovery process more efficient. In fact, by combining asset discovery with network maps from teams responsible for the systems on the target networks it is possible to uncover potential security threats relatively quickly. Almost every organization of any size has orphaned systems somewhere on the network, such as a server that hosts a tool that was once widely used and is now abandoned, but not properly decommissioned, or an old VPN concentrator that is no longer in use, because it does not meet current encryption standards. There are many examples of different types of orphaned systems throughout large networks. By comparing notes from the asset discovery tool with information collected from the various teams it is possible to quickly identify orphaned systems in the network. The security team can then work with the different groups to make sure these systems are properly decommissioned and removed from the network.

Between the asset discovery process and the interview process a security team can build a relatively accurate network map that includes systems on the network, the purpose of those systems, and who is responsible for control over those systems. Not only does having this data give the security team a better understanding of the entire network, it is also necessary for compliance purposes within many organizations.

Most networks are extremely dynamic – new systems are constantly being provisioned and old systems removed, user laptops are assigned a new IP address every time they connect to the DHCP (Dynamic Host Configuration Protocol) server, and so on. The point is, the network map that the security team just spent weeks building will very quickly become obsolete. To keep it up-to-date and populated with current information, asset discovery needs to be performed on a regular basis. For organizations that are just building a network security program, asset discovery can be a weekly, or even a monthly, process. As organizations move closer to continuous monitoring, asset discovery scans should be running constantly. The more often they are run, the better the security team is able to maintain situational awareness around changes to the network.

As with the initial scan, continuously running asset scans are not run in a vacuum, there is a reason why a system may have gone offline, or a new system come online. That is where the relationships within the rest of the organization developed during the interview process are so important. Rather than spending half the day hunting down who the owner of a system or network is, the security team can reach out to the named owner to find out why a system went offline or what the purpose of the new system is. Taking the process to the next level, groups within the organization can even proactively notify the security team. This way, the security knows in advance when changes are being made to the systems and can make appropriate notations.

Remember that asset discovery and asset management in an intelligence-led security program is about more than just knowing what is on the network. An intelligence-led security team also needs to understand the purpose of the systems on the network, and rate those systems based on the criticality to the organization. In its simplest form, there are certain systems that are almost always deemed critical inside a network: Domain Controller, Mail Sever, File Server, Database Server, Web Server, and so on. These assets should be rated critical in the organization. But there may be other assets specific to an organization that also should be labeled critical. For example, some security teams consider the laptops/desktops of organizational leaders to be critical assets. Which is why, to be effective, the security teams in an intelligence-led organization need to understand every aspect of the business. Conversely, it also explains why different groups within the organization need to understand the security plan and should be involved in the process of building it out.

Collected asset data should be stored someplace where it can be regularly accessed, monitored, and acted upon as needed. This usually involves a Governance, Risk, and Compliance (GRC) tool. A GRC tool, such as LockPath's Keylight™ (www.lockpath.com) and RSA's Archer (www.rsa.com), allows an organization to collect scanned data from various tools and correlate that data with other collected data from within the organization. GRCs have traditionally been thought of as a compliance tool – a one-stop shop that allows compliance teams to instantly pull information requested by auditors to show compliance. But in an intelligence-led security organization, they serve a larger purpose. By correlating asset-discovery information with known vulnerabilities and configurations, information security teams can prioritize risk to the organization and schedule patching maintenance windows based on a risk score, rather than on whatever the scare of the day is.

A GRC tool is really the first step in moving toward an intelligence-led security program, because the GRC allows an organization to apply its own risk rating to a discovered vulnerability. A security team that relies solely on a traditional scanning tool only has the criticality rating the scanning tool provides to help determine patching priority. By pulling the scanning data in to a GRC data that data can be correlated with other network information to determine a customized patching priority that is relevant to the assets in the organization. For example a critical vulnerability on a server in a lab that is disconnected from the rest of the network is likely a lower

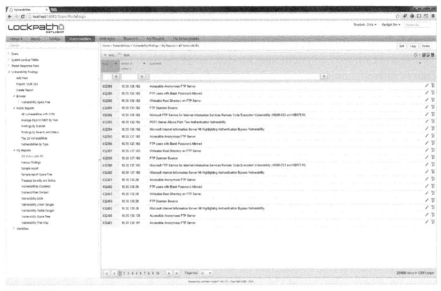

FIGURE 5.1

Reporting vulnerabilities by IP address in LockPath's Keylight.

priority to patch than a moderate vulnerability on a server that contains customer credit card information. Risk can be assigned based on a number of factors, including where the system sits in the network (Figure 5.1), what type of data is on the system, and whether or not there is a public exploit for the vulnerability. The last point can be very important for determining patching priorities, especially for the publicly facing server. A vulnerability with no known public exploits is almost always a lower patch priority than a vulnerability that has an exploit that has been converted to a module.

A GRC allows organizations to build this customized risk framework by providing a variety of network insights in a single location. Many organizations rely on the Open Web Application Security Project (OWASP) (www.owasp.org) framework for determining risk. In its simplest form, OWASP uses a standard equation for determining risk:

$$\text{Risk} = \text{Likelihood} \times \text{Impact}$$

Using this equation, each organization can look at a vulnerability based on the likelihood that it will be exploited within the organization's network and the impact that exploitation of the vulnerability would have on the organization. The OWASP model turns vulnerability scanning and patching from a strictly technical discussion to a business discussion. It allows a security team to prioritize patching based on business impact and to explain the costs of vulnerability management in terms that organizational leaders understand.

A GRC also feeds into the intelligence cycle. A GRC serves as a collection point for information from a variety of sources, both internal and external to the organization. The data within the GRC is analyzed and used to produce reports that are disseminated to those within the organization who need them. Remember the definition of cyber threat intelligence from Chapter 3 (see p. 40):

> *Evidence-based knowledge, including context, mechanisms, indicators, implications, and actionable advice, about an existing or emerging menace or hazard to assets that can be used to inform decisions regarding the subject's response to that menace or hazard. (McMillan, 2013)*

By collecting asset vulnerability data and correlating that information to organizational priorities – knowing what the organization at large considers a critical asset – an organization is taking the first step toward becoming an intelligence led security organization. In fact, most organizations begin the move toward the Intelligence-Guided Computer Network Defense (IGCND) model at the vulnerability level.

It is important to note here that although GRC tools serve a valuable security purpose, they are still viewed by many as primarily a compliance tool, another function that they do very well. Because most organizations separate compliance and security functions, part of the security strategy planning will involve how to enable both compliance and security organizations to make the most use of the existing platform.

The good news is that most GRC vendors have recognized their value as a security tool and provide different modules, templates, and views, depending on the role of the person logging into the console. There is no reason to invest in a new platform when a few tweaks to the existing platform will allow both functions to peacefully coexist.

CONFIGURATION MANAGEMENT

To this point the discussion has revolved around the external-facing configuration of systems on the network. But that is not enough. Vulnerabilities don't just exist in external-facing applications that can be detected via network scan. In fact, most exploitations occur through applications that cannot be accessed externally. Security teams not only need to make sure that the most recent server daemons are installed on servers, but they also need to ensure that desktops in the network are running the latest versions of Adobe PDF Reader, Microsoft Word, Google Chrome, and other desktop applications.

Tools such as Symantec's Altiris and IBM's Tivoli are useful for understanding what software is installed on the network. These tools allow a compliance team to quickly understand what is installed and ensure that the organization is in license compliance, and that there are no rogue programs installed on the network.

But endpoint management software serves more than just a compliance purpose. Given the threat desktop applications can pose to the security of the network, the security team can also use the information collected through endpoint management tools to improve the security of the network.

Many security analysts understand, at a high level, that PDFs have the potential to be bad, but don't necessarily understand how an attacker goes from PDF to compromised system. There are really three parts to a PDF exploit: embedded JavaScript, memory-resident shell code, and the exploit itself.

Depending on the version of Adobe Reader running in the network, there are a number of known buffer overflows that an attacker can exploit (no pun intended). The attacker needs to either create or steal a PDF that is of interest to the attacker's target. In addition to the content, the attacker loads a JavaScript that contains both the exploit and the shell code.

When the victim opens the PDF document, the JavaScript executes automatically – Adobe Reader has its own web engine. The JavaScript calls the exploit code, which crashes Adobe Reader and runs the shell code in memory. The attacker now has control of the target system and can download and install whatever permanent tools the attacker prefers. More sophisticated versions of the PDF exploit restart the Adobe Reader instantly so the target does not become suspicious.

It seems like an easy way to prevent these types of attacks is to disable JavaScript within Adobe Reader, but that disables legitimate functionality for a lot of users. Security is about protecting the organization while providing as much functionality as possible to users. Finding the right compromise can sometimes be a challenge.

As with external scanning, asset management tools allow the security team to compare the list of software installed on systems throughout the network against known vulnerabilities. When new vulnerabilities are identified, the security team can use to determine the priority in which these systems will be patched. Again, by taking data from the endpoint management system and integrating that data with asset discovery data into a GRC tool, endpoint patch management can be prioritized alongside system patch management.

Endpoint management tools serve another security function: They can help security teams uncover rogue programs in their networks, whether those programs were installed wittingly or not. Endpoint management tools look for new applications being installed and can be configured to report those automatically, which allows the security team to examine those files to determine if they are safe or not.

Of course, in an ideal world users would know better than to install a rogue application without having it reviewed by the security team. The truth is that many users don't think about the consequences of the applications they install. This is especially true for mobile devices. Many organizations assign their users smart phones or allow users to use their own smart phones for work purposes. Given the rampant malware-posing-as-apps in the smartphone ecosystem, this can be a security nightmare.

One alternative is to use these same endpoint management systems to track what apps are being installed on the phones, and verify that no known rogue apps are installed (given the rapid proliferation of rogue apps, even on legitimate app stores, this can be a challenge in and of itself). The other option is to create an internal app store, which can only be accessed by employees. This limits the apps that users can access on their organization-connected smart phone, and also provides better security for the organization at large.

Not all rogue applications are installed wittingly, if a user is compromised and the attacker installs malware, endpoint management tools can help detect that rogue application. Endpoint management tools are not antivirus or malware-detection platforms, so they will not detect based on signature or behavior. Instead, these programs simply tell the security team that something is now on the system that was not there before. It could be a new process or a newly installed program, but if an organization is engaging in proper configuration management, the security team should detect that something new is installed and investigate.

Being able to investigate every system file change is not realistic for most organizations, which is why security teams do not generally rely on asset management tools for incident response. However, knowing what a system looks like, and being able to quickly identify when there are changes to a system – even if the identification is done retroactively—does provide a powerful tool in the arsenal of the security team.

Endpoint management tools also help to ensure that all systems on the network meet the minimum requirements established by the security baseline. Of course, to meet those requirements the security team has to first establish security baseline. The security baseline should consist of a list of approved tools/applications for use in the organization, and the minimum acceptable version for each of those tools. The security baseline is a living document that changes as software is updated, added to, or removed from the network.

Using an endpoint management tool, the security team can enforce compliance with the security baseline. Many of these tools will even push software updates to the endpoints. This helps to maintain consistency across the network and the tools can be used to provide running reports of users that are in compliance with the security baseline, and more importantly out of compliance.

As with asset discovery, using endpoint management tools to report on compliance with the security baseline should be a continuous process – the more often compliance reports are run, the easier it is to track down and fix an out-of-compliance system and the better the situational awareness of the security team. Also, as with asset discovery, endpoint management allows security teams to match the latest reported threats against their system information and prioritize patching. For example, if a new critical Adobe Reader vulnerability is discovered along with proof-of-concept exploit code, rather than having to wade through all of the workstations and servers on the network to find out who has which version installed, an endpoint management tool enables the security team to run a single report and have an instant view of the organization's exposure to this new vulnerability. Having this information, along with an understanding of how critical Adobe Reader is to the day-to-day operations of the organization, the security team can now make a risk-informed, intelligence-driven decision on what actions need to be taken. The security team can now present this decision in business terms: "This vulnerability presents a high-risk to our organization because there is an exploit in the wild, and 60% of our systems are vulnerable. Temporarily disabling access to PDF files will cost the organization $120,000 in lost productivity."

Configuration management also includes the management of the configuration of network devices such as firewalls, routers, switches, Web proxies, and more. Firewall configuration management is especially critical to a security team, in order to have an immediate understanding of what traffic is allowed into and out of the network.

Using a tool like SolarWinds (www.solarwinds.com) gives security teams the ability to not only maintain backups of the configuration of network devices, but also to understand, at a glance, what the configuration of those devices looks like.

NETWORK LOGGING

In most organizations either allowed logs to collect on the individual systems or they collected those logs on a centralized Syslog server. Given the explosion in security devices on the network since then, a simple Syslog server is not enough and most organizations have migrated to a Security Information and Event Management (SIEM) tool. SIEMs, such as ArcSight (www.hp.com) and Splunk (www.splunk.com), allow organizations to collect logs from sources throughout the network, correlate those logs, and produce security events. A SIEM is a great tool because it allows security events from a variety of security systems to present themselves in a single console. No more jumping from console to console to track a security event; instead, events from multiple sources can be instantly tracked by time of incident, username, IP address, domain name, and much more.

A well-managed SIEM environment allows a security team to maintain situational awareness over the network. It provides immediate visibility into firewall, Intrusion Detection System (IDS), proxy, endpoint alerts, and more. With the right rules, a SIEM correlates those collected logs to present security events to the security team. Unfortunately, a poorly managed SIEM can exasperate the biggest problem that security teams face today: too many events with no prioritization of those events and not enough time to properly deal with them all.

THE TROUBLE WITH SIEMs

SIEMs are without a doubt an invaluable security tool, but they have their shortcomings. Already mentioned is that SIEMs often make more work for security teams, rather than less. The reason for this is the nature of the SIEM environment. The SIEM, by design, simply reports events delivered from the logs of third-party sources. If a firewall sends a security event that it rates as critical, the SIEM processes it as a critical event. The same applies to events from endpoint security solutions, Web proxies, and more. In a typical day, that adds up to hundreds of "critical" security events from devices across the network, all of which are presented equally inside the SIEM console.

Experienced security professionals know that not all "critical" security events are created equal. A critical alert from the IDS that matches against known Gameover ZeuS traffic is a higher priority than an alert from the McAfee ePO server saying it has quarantined a well-known and widely deployed variant of Qakbot. So, even though both are classified as critical, only one really is. Unfortunately, if that one is at the bottom of the queue behind a myriad of noncritical critical alerts, it might not be dealt with until the malware has embedded itself on several machines.

One way to solve this problem is through the use of intelligence. By applying an intelligence overlay to the SIEM environment, a security team is better able to prioritize these critical events. The right kind of intelligence can help security teams prioritize events based on the risk presented specifically to the organization. This will be discussed in greater depth in the next chapter.

There are ways to improve the efficiency of a SIEM installation, without adding the external intelligence overlay. In fact, these steps should be taken before adding external intelligence.

First, it is important to take a step back and ensure that not only are logs being collected from the right systems, but that they are being collected at the right level. Fortunately, building upon the previous work done around asset discovery, the organization should have a complete and accurate picture of what systems exist on the network. So, step one is to ensure that the list of devices that are sending logs to the SIEM matches up with the list of systems identified in the GRC. If there are systems that are not sending logs, determine why that is and take steps to account for those systems.

Log collection is not necessarily a one-to-one process and the configuration information for each of those systems also needs to be considered. For example, a server may be running Red Hat Enterprise Linux, so the operating system logs should be sent to the SIEM. That same system may also be running an Oracle server, so the database logs should also be sent to the SIEM – two sets of logs from the same server but serving different purposes. Conversely, it is entirely reasonable that an organization may not collect any logs directly from desktop systems, instead relying on the installed antivirus program to grab the needed information and send those logs to the vendor's console. Rather than having hundreds or thousands of desktops send logs, the logs can batched at the console and forwarded from the console to the SIEM.[1]

Application logs are as critical as the system logs, which is why it is important to understand the function of each system on the network. That means understanding not just what the asset scan reveals but how the owners of the system use it. Not every application generates logs and not every application that generates logs produces security data that is actionable. Generally speaking, desktop applications do not provide any actionable security information, whereas server applications provide more robust logging that can be actionable.

For system or application log to be effective, it must log at a level that provides enough information for the security team to be able to act upon a security event. A "critical" security event that does not provide actionable information for the security team is a waste of time. Actionable information is anything that starts to provide the context security teams need to make a decision, something that the security team can pivot from to enhance the security of the network.

For example, if a security program reports that it found a suspicious file with the hash 8731bc3ab7ac24e0baed1d6772d2bbea, but doesn't provide information regarding what systems the file was found on or the associated file name, then it hasn't done anything to improve the security posture of the network. A security log should

---

[1]Ensure that the logs collected by the antivirus vendor meet both security and compliance requirements.

always provide at least some level of context around the event. To be effective, a security log, at a minimum, should include a timestamp, source and destination IP addresses, source and destination ports, a customized criticality rating, and an explanation of the alert. There are some exceptions to this rule, but not many – these details allow for correlation against other systems on the network so as to build a big picture of what has happened.

This correlation is where SIEMs, when they have the right information, really shine. A SIEM with the right log data and the right filters in place is a big step in moving away from "Whack-a-Mole" security. In a well-run SIEM environment, a security analyst can correlate an attack on a workstation with the domain information collected from the proxy and any attempts to call out to a command and control host through the firewall. Now, instead of just wiping the workstation and reinstalling the operating system, the security team can put blocks in place at the proxy and the firewall to prevent the attack from recurring, or infecting other users on the network.

Connecting the dots in this manner is part of the power of SIEMs, but it is also one of their downsides. The capabilities of the SIEM often mean that it is hard to configure properly. Collecting data is easy, but the rules that connect one dataset to another can be challenging. Many SIEM providers offer out-of-the-box filtering rules that assist most organizations as they are getting started, but because each network is unique with its own security needs, those rules often don't go far enough. When they aren't enough, the options are to figure out how to write filtering rules that will work for the organization or bring in a consultant who can help write those rules. Again, many security teams are hesitant to bring in consultants, but this is another case where it is probably worth it, especially if there is not someone on staff with the necessary expertise. The SIEM can be one of the most powerful tools at the disposal of the security team; there is no reason not to have it running at peak efficiency.

In addition to correlation rules, a SIEM has to be tuned so that not every security event sent to it is listed as a high priority. Some of that tuning needs to be done on the systems that are sending the logs to the SIEM. Whenever possible, adjust the source logging to accurately reflect criticality that events from system are actually rated. When these changes cannot be made at the source, the security team can write rules that automatically adjust down certain events and raise other events.

In the Qakbot example used previously, a quarantined piece of commodity malware is usually not considered a critical event, but if that same event happened across 20 desktops in the span of 10 minutes, suddenly there might be a critical event and it is worth raising the severity level within the SIEM.

THE POWER OF SIEMs

A SIEM is, obviously, a very powerful tool. There are things a SIEM, with the right rules in place, can do to detect security incidents that are not caught by other security tools natively.

One area in which SIEMs excel is correlation of events across an entire network. This capability was hinted at earlier, but it is worth exploring this idea in more detail. For the most part, security tools identify potential security events in a vacuum, with no context, even if an event is detected across multiple sources from the same security devices. For example, an IDS detects suspicious traffic emanating from a workstation, it then detects the same type of traffic from 20 other workstations. Within the IDS console each event is treated as a unique incident and not tied to the other 20 incidents (this is not always the case; some IDS vendors have very advanced consoles). A quick glance at the console shows that there is an outbreak, but unless someone is looking at the console, the outbreak can continue to spread throughout the network.

Within a SIEM console the security team can write rules that will trigger different alerts depending on the frequency of the occurrence. Twenty-one similar events from the IDS in the span of a few minutes can trigger a rule that automatically sends SMS (short message service) messages to everyone in security.

That seems like an obvious example, but this capability can be used to trigger nonobvious events. Using the attack above, but this time the attacker is a professional and operating in low-and-slow mode. The attacker knocks over one desktop, waits a few days, then knocks over the second one, and so on. It takes the attacker two months to gain access to the same 21 machines. Now a human staring at the IDS console may not notice the pattern, as there are a lot of other events occurred between each of these 21 specific events. Again, there is no reason that a SIEM rule cannot be written looking for certain activity over a longer period of time and alerting the security team when a certain threshold is met within that timeframe. Of course, these alerts cannot be made on every type of alert; they need to be tuned to only those alerts that represent the greatest threats to the organization. Knowing the type of adversaries who are targeting the organization and their preferred tools and infrastructure helps to prioritize which rules should be written to alert over longer periods of time.

It goes without saying that SIEMs can alert on low-and-slow events that occur across multiple security systems on the network. Let's say an attacker uses a phishing email to compromise several employees. The domain and message pass through the mail server and are logged, the payload passes through either the proxy or the Web Application Firewall (WAF) and a piece of malware is installed on the desktop. Information about all of these activities is logged, and most likely generates an alert somewhere along the way. These systems may sit quietly for days or weeks before calling out, and when they do call out, they are going to call out to servers that are related to the infrastructure used in the attack. Of course, the connection between the attack infrastructure and the command and control infrastructure may not be immediately obvious (though it often is). This is an area where third-party intelligence can prove especially useful. Knowing the related infrastructure can mean that while the adversary successfully penetrated the network, the adversary is unable to call out and cause any further damage, effectively turning the network into a roach motel.

Even logs that do not appear to be an immediate security event, can present a threat. Again, using the right rules within the SIEM, even a seemingly harmless series of logs can be correlated and presented as a security event. Take the example of Domain Name System (DNS) tunneling. DNS tunneling has had a bit of resurgence as a command and control (C&C) communication method. This is done out of necessity. Web proxies have gotten a lot better at detecting malicious URL traffic, and it is harder to trick them into allowing C&C traffic through (though HTTP/HTTPS are still the most common form of C&C traffic). DNS tunneling encodes C&C traffic in DNS requests. An attacker may encode commands or small exfiltration as an A Record request. The malware may send a DNS request for zdsefgsfgrghrt.example.com that triggers a response from the C&C server that contains commands encoded as a TXT response or one of the many other responses. All of this traffic travels from the infected machine, through the infected organization's DNS server, out to the C&C server, which sends the response back to the organization's DNS server[2] where it gets forwarded back to the original infected workstation. In other words, it operates just like a standard DNS query, because it is.

The problem with DNS tunneling is that there is a limit to the size of the queries and responses that are supported within the DNS protocol. Effective DNS tunneling, especially if exfiltration is involved, requires a lot of DNS packets to be sent through the network. Fortunately, for the adversary using this technique, very few organizations monitor DNS traffic to the level they should. This means that DNS tunneling can be a highly effective method for getting data out of a locked down network without being detected.

Unless, of course, that organization has implemented the right SIEM rules to detect DNS tunneling. Remember that the DNS server logs every one of these queries, so a rule that alerts when uncommon DNS records, like PTR or AAAA, are made will catch this type of activity. A rule that alerts whenever a certain threshold of queries to the same domain name from the same machine in the network is made (e.g. 1000 queries in 10 minutes) will also stop this type of traffic.

SIEMs are also useful for creating alerts based on anomalous traffic. As with the DNS example above, anomalous traffic is traffic that, on the surface, appears to be legitimate but doesn't fit within the context of the organization. For example, port 25 (SMTP) traffic is generally considered legitimate traffic when it is originating from the mail server, but it is probably not legitimate traffic if it is originating from an internal file server. A SIEM can be configured to be alert when traffic originating from a system is different from older traffic patterns. A SIEM can also be configured to alert if legitimate and historically accurate traffic suddenly increases or decreases exponentially. A Web server that has been generating a fairly consistent number of logs over the last 90 days suddenly starts generating 10 times the normal number of logs. This may be a sign of a compromised host being used to launch attacks against other hosts. By using SIEM rules, a security team can receive different levels of alerts depending on the standard deviation of traffic. Five standard deviations may result in an alert being sent to the console, whereas a 10–standard deviation in traffic may result in an SMS message being sent.

Successful anomalous traffic detection requires an understanding of the network. Each of these security components builds on the one before it. If the network is not properly mapped and the role of the systems on the network not well documented, then anomalous traffic detection is extremely difficult. To know what is out of the ordinary, it is necessary to first understand what is expected behavior.

---

[2]A few steps in the DNS process are skipped here for brevity's sake.

MANAGED SECURITY SERVICE PROVIDERS

Some organizations are simply not equipped to manage log collection in-house. There may not be enough staff, enough money in the budget, or the technical expertise is simply not there. In cases where network log collection is not an option, a Managed Security Service Provider (MSSP) can be an excellent alternative.

MSSPs perform many of the same functions of a SIEM, in fact, many use a local SIEM as a log aggregator, but they handle the correlation and log or event storage in the cloud. MSSPs such as eSentire (www.esentire.com), Dell SecureWorks (www.secureworks.com), Symantec Managed Security Services (www.symantec.com), and Verizon Managed Security Services (www.verizonenterprise.com) provide customers with prioritized alerts that allow organizations to rapidly respond to those security incidents that present the greatest threat to the organization.

As with SIEMs, MSSPs track events over time and can help organizations understand how the threats to their organization have changed. Using query capabilities of the MSSP portal, and customized rules an MSSP customer can track repeat infections, receive anomalous traffic alerts, and get a better understanding of the threats posed to their organization, all of which can be nicely displayed within the MSSP portal, similar to Figure 5.2.

One of the bestselling points of an MSSP is that the MSSP serves a lot of clients around the world in a variety of verticals. The MSSP sees a lot of surface attack data from all of those customers, which gives the MSSP insight into trending threats and attack methods that most organizations do not have.

In other words, the MSSP has a certain level of external intelligence that the organizations they are serving do not have. They can use that intelligence to alert on events that may seem like normal traffic to the organizations they serve. For example, an MSSP has a client that is infected with a new version of Trojan.Agent.BDSA that

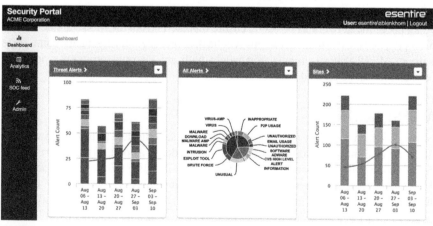

FIGURE 5.2

eSentire security portal.

calls out to domain that was not previously associated with this malware. The MSSP has now identified the domain and associated it with this particular piece of malware. Now, every time a system on a client network attempts to call out to this domain, the MSSP not only knows to alert on it, but the MSSP can also tell its customer what malware to look for and the steps the customer needs to take to remove the malware from the network.

In effect, the MSSP has applied both operational and tactical intelligence to the traffic it is collecting from its customers. Operationally, it can tell the customer that a specific domain is bad, and tactically, it can tell the customer the tools associated with the activity.

Although an MSSP is a powerful tool, it is just that. The MSSP cannot take the place of an organization's security program. The MSSP can be a component, and in some cases even a full partner, of the security program, but it cannot be the only part of it.

No matter how good an MSSP is, it will never understand an organization's network as well as the organization. Using an MSSP is most effective when an organization has done all of the prep worked described earlier in the chapter. Understanding the assets in the network that are sending logs to the MSSP is even more critical to ensure that the criticality of the alerts from the MSSP match up with the criticality of the assets within the network. To that end, there is generally a learning period of six months or so where the MSSP is gathering knowledge of the organization's network and trying to understand the organization's risk profile.

Ideally, alerts that are generated from the MSSP should be checked against other data sources within the network, and there should be a constant feedback loop going between the organization and the MSSP to ensure that event criticality is being properly set.

If an organization decides that an MSSP is the best fit for its security program, the same planning that goes into building an in-house security program should be applied to the MSSP. The organization should work with the MSSP to determine which logs will provide the most security value, provide the MSSP with as much detail about the network as possible, ensure that alerts from the MSSP are dealt with promptly, and ensure that continuous feedback is provided. By taking the same steps with an MSSP that an organization would with any security program a powerful partnership can be created.

ACCESS CONTROL

Network systems are not the only assets that the security team has to be aware of; there are also human assets that have to be considered as part of the security plan. Access control is the process of ensuring that only those employees or partners who have a need for access to a system or data are granted access to that system or data. As with asset management, access control involves understanding the network at large. A security team needs to understand the role of groups, and the users in those groups, within the organization so as to better understand the systems and files to which they need access.

Many organizations have networks that are very flat, which means that users from one group are visible to systems belonging to another group. A quick network scan from a user desktop can essentially map the entire network, providing an attacker with valuable to data to expand an attack.

Whenever possible, groups should be segmented within the network. The sales team does not need to have access to engineering systems and human resources does not need access to marketing systems. Using VLANs (virtual local area networks) and other segmenting tools, the security team can help limit the damage to other parts of the network from the source of the infection. The other advantage of a segmented network design is that it forces traffic to flow through the security systems in the network.

Logically, where do most security systems sit in the network? They sit at the edge, which means that an attacker who manages to compromise a user's desktop and disable any endpoint security applications on the machine has free reign within the network with very little chance of being detected. Conversely, a segmented network will force all traffic out of that segment to traverse through a set of core switches, which is an easy place to setup an IDS specially tuned to detect machine-to-machine malicious activity on a span port.

Access control also involves understanding the patterns of access that users have into and within the network. This type of understanding includes, for example, knowing when a user is on vacation, so a VPN connection from that user that originates in France isn't as alarming as one from an unknown user. It also means knowing which users are administrators, and closely monitoring their activity, especially afterhours activity.

Although no one in the security business wants to be involved in human resources activity, the fact is that users present the biggest cyber security threat to the organization. Understanding how users behave on the network and alerting when there is a significant variation in that activity can protect the organization from insider threats as well as malicious actors posing as legitimate users.

As a general rule, attackers want to take the path of least resistance to gain access to their target data. Even though the attacker may have a wide range of exploit tools at their disposal, there is an inherent risk of discovery with every exploit attempted. That begs the question: Why exploit when it is easier just to impersonate a user, especially if that user is an administrator? Once an attacker has successfully penetrated a network, the most common avenue for moving around that network is to grab an administrator's credentials and use those to jump from machine to machine and install the malware. Which is why monitoring access patterns is so critical for securing the network. Access patterns provide context to the activity in which the user is engaging. If an administrator who primarily works with Linux servers is suddenly logging into one Microsoft Windows workstation after another, that may indicate suspicious behavior.

Most organizations rely on Microsoft Active Directory to handle authentication and to define user groups within the network. Active Directory information should be sent to the SIEM, or, if possible, to the MSSP, because user activity can serve as a pivot against other logs that show activity by the user. Tracking access information and movement from the network with a SIEM, combined with an understanding of that user's role within the organization, helps the security team determine whether an activity is malicious or part of the normal pattern of behavior.

NETWORK MONITORING

The big flaw with both the SIEM and the MSSP log collection models is that they alert the security team after an incident has happened. That doesn't change their value. It is just that they force the security team to always be reactive, when one of the major advantages of an intelligence-led organization is the ability to be reactive. There are some ways to mitigate this, which are discussed in Chapter 6, but overall SIEMs and MSSP are postevent diagnostic tools.

Network monitoring involves more than simply signature based IDS monitoring. While an IDS certainly serves a purpose, generally an alert from an IDS only provides the signature information. As an organization matures, its security program using network security monitors like Bro (www.bro.org), R-Scope (www.reservoir.com), and Lancope (www.lancope.com) can improve the responsiveness of the security team to the point where attacks can be stopped in progress.

Network security monitors capture all traffic flowing through the network and they look for patterns that are indicative of a security event. These are not signatures in the traditional sense; instead they are looking for behavior that indicates malware is happening. An example of this might be a piece of malware that is trying to use port 443 (SSL) for exfiltration, but the traffic does not match what traffic over port 443 should look like. The network security monitor can alert to the suspicious traffic without any signatures in place.

Most of these tools have the ability to analyze network traffic using a wide variety of methods. Protocol analysis, as outlined above, is one of the most common methods. Malware authors are often sloppy in their implementation of protocols within the malware, so monitoring for packets that seem malformed is an easy way to look for a potentially unknown threat.

Network monitoring tools can also monitor for suspicious behavior such as large file transfers, or file transfers late at night. They can monitor for attempted access to sensitive servers, as in Figure 5.3, which shows a SSH (secure socket shell) brute-force attempt.

Of course, the server is also going to log this information and present it to the SIEM, but the alert may not be picked up until much later. Using network monitoring tools, it is possible for the security team to catch an attack live, and stop it as it is happening.

Just as with all of the other components of security, to have effective live network monitoring there needs to be context around the threats to the network.

Effective network logging builds upon effective asset and configuration management and effective network monitoring builds on both components. Most network

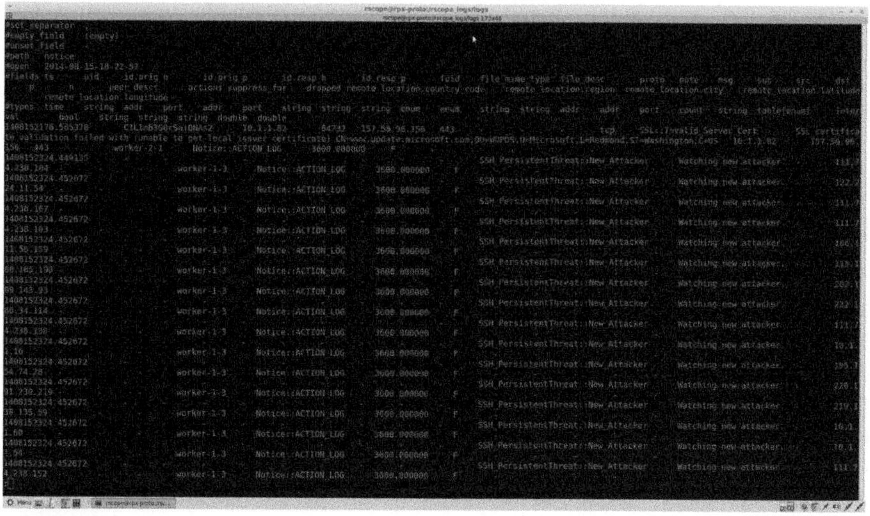

FIGURE 5.3

Reservoir Labs R-Scope capturing a brute force attempt.

monitoring tools feed directly into a SIEM or can send logs directly to the MSSP, because in addition to being effective at stopping live attacks, they also provide a rich data source for correlation against other systems in the network. In fact, they can be a valuable forensics tool for an analyst trying to investigate an attack, or conduct a postmortem. Most systems on the network provide log information that only presents a snapshot of what happened during the exact time an event occurred. That snapshot does not provide any context as to what happened before or after that event. Analysts can often put together the puzzle by correlating against other logs from the same system or logs from other systems that have related event information. But a network monitor is designed to capture all traffic, all the time, almost like a TiVo for the network. It allows the security team to review a full packet capture of what happened before the event and immediately following the event.

Although providing postevent support is an important function of network monitors, the primary role is providing real-time situational awareness to the security team about potential security incidents occurring on the network.

To provide the most effective coverage, there should be multiple network monitors strategically placed around the network. The goal is not to capture all traffic on the network; instead, the goal is to capture traffic that will provide the greatest security benefit to the network. Of course, as with any security device, to prevent the security team from being overwhelmed with alerts from a network monitor, the systems need to tuned so that they are presenting only alerts that are critical to the organization and that present an immediate threat. A well-tuned network monitoring system will only provide a few critical alerts each day, but those alerts will be the ones that are most critical to the organization.

One way to enhance the capability of network monitors is through intelligence. By providing specific pivot points, such as IP addresses, domain names, and file hashes, that the networking monitoring system can watch for, it helps to filter out the potential false-positives and correlate the collected data against intelligence feeds. There is further discussion of this in Chapter 6.

CONCLUSION

As the old saying goes, "you must learn to walk before you can run." The same is true with security. Organizations that attempt to jump right into building an intelligence-led security program without first taking care of the basics are doomed to failure.

The basics of a solid security program means continuous monitoring of all aspects of security within the network. It starts at the bottom with an understanding of what assets are on the network and what role each of those assets serves. Once the core understanding is present, the next phase is to continuously monitor those systems for changes, combining the asset-monitoring information with information about new vulnerabilities that are applicable to systems in the organization's network.

The next component of a strong security framework is collecting and monitoring logs from systems on the network. At a minimum, logs should be collected from firewalls, IDSs, proxies, mail servers, WAFs, servers, and endpoint protection systems.

Collecting the logs is only the first step. Once the logs are collected and live inside a SIEM or reside in the cloud at an MSSP, they need to be correlated against logs from the other systems. Rules have to be developed to use that log information to produce actionable security events that can easily be prioritized and addressed based on a situational awareness of the systems that being impacted by those events.

Once the logs are in place and relevant security rules are written, the next step is to move from a reactive security posture to a proactive one. One way to get a jump on that is by using a finely tuned network monitor to stop attacks against critical systems as they happen. Network monitors allow for real-time packet capture of security incidents, so they make a great forensics tool. More importantly, they provide real-time situational awareness of malicious activity occurring on the network. Using the alerts with the packet capture information, a security team can easily take steps to stop an attack in progress and prevent the attack from reoccurring.

The focus of this chapter was the context and improved security that can be gained just by connecting the dots from the systems within the network. This is a basic form of intelligence that can greatly improve the security of an organization. This chapter started with a quote from Sun Tzu, "If you know the enemy and know yourself, you need not fear the result of a hundred battles." This chapter was all about "knowing yourself." In Chapter 6, it is time to "know the enemy."

REFERENCES

McMillan, R., 2013. Definition: threat intelligence. <https://www.gartner.com/doc/2487216/ definition-threat-intelligence> (accessed 27.07.14.).

Tzu, S., The Art of War, (Lionel Giles, Trans.). Polity, New York, p. 11.

External intelligence sources

6

INFORMATION IN THIS CHAPTER:

- Brand monitoring versus intelligence
- Asset, vulnerability, and configuration management
- Network logging
- Network monitoring
- Protecting against zero-day attacks
- Incident response and intelligence
- Collaborative research into threats (CRITs)

INTRODUCTION

Now the fun starts. Fun may seem like a strange term to use when security teams are fighting a losing against an onslaught of attacks against every part of the network and from around the world. Good intelligence, properly applied, can help to shift the battle in favor of the organization. No security team is going to be perfect – there are too many threats to catch all of them – but with the proper intelligence and vendor support an intelligence-led security organization is better prepared to deal with a breach.

It is important to note that any security framework is going to assume at some point the organization will be breached and the security plan should account for that eventuality. Consequently, part of building an intelligence-led security organization is having a plan for dealing with a breach and testing that plan often. Just as network teams regularly test backup systems and infrastructure teams regularly test UPS (uninterrupted power supply) and generator support, the ability of the security team, or, if it is separate, the incident response team, to effectively respond to a breach should be challenged.

Chapter 5 (see p. 77) focused on situational awareness surrounding the network. To effectively secure the organization, the security team first has to understand the organization. The goal of this chapter is to switch focus from the internal to the external. Collecting data from third-party sources and correlating that data against the data collected within the organization is what ultimately creates finished, actionable intelligence that is specific the organization.

Sometimes collecting external data that is relative to an organization is easy: a post to Pastebin (www.pastebin.com) or a Tweet (www.twitter.com) mentioning a planned Distributed Denial of Service (DDoS) attack against the organization. Some of this data is more difficult to collect; for example, a group from China testing new tools against targets in Bangladesh prior to launching a campaign against companies in the United States. The point is that this external information can have a direct impact on the security of the organization and can help shape the security precautions that an organization will take to protect itself.

Understanding a threat in terms of the three tiers of intelligence – strategic, tactical, and operational – helps to improve situational awareness of both the internal state of the organization and the external threats to that organization.

The goal of this chapter is to help security teams fuse external information to their internal intelligence cycle. Remember that while many vendors tout their intelligence capabilities, what they are really providing is additional information designed to correlate against data collected within the network to determine a course of action. Until the information provided by the vendor is deemed actionable, it is just data. It is intelligence only when it is relevant to the organization.

BRAND MONITORING VERSUS INTELLIGENCE

Organizations making the move from "Whack-a-Mole" security to Intelligence-Guided Computer and Network Defense (IGCND) often conflate brand monitoring with intelligence. Brand monitoring can be an important part of IGCND, and certainly understanding the perception of an organization and people making threats against the organization is important, but it is not necessarily intelligence.

Consider, for example, the everpresent #opWhatever on Twitter. It seems almost daily that one group or another is announcing a different "operation" against a sector or specific organization. It is usually fronted with a hashtag and consists of threats to use their all-powerful army to launch DDoS attacks against the target du jour.

An organization's name being included as part of one of these operations is not necessarily intelligence, though it is a valuable data point. The intelligence in this case revolves around the group and the potential danger it poses. Sometimes these attacks are simply hashtags and nothing else. The group may be newly formed with poor capabilities, or it may not be a group at all, it may simply be someone trying to gain Twitter followers by making outlandish claims. On the other hand, the group may have a long history of successfully launching these types of campaigns. In that case, it is important to gain a strategic and tactical understanding of how they operate. What tools do they use? What parts of the organization do they tend to launch their DDoS attacks against? How long can they keep up a sustained attack?

Both sets of information are valuable. Knowing that a threat is most likely an empty one means that the security team does not need to be spun up and placed on 24×7 alert until the threat passes. Conversely, knowing a threat is real and understanding the adversary's tactics enables the security team to properly test countermeasures and warn network users, and possibly customers, of the threat.

Organizations that are going to engage in brand monitoring alongside intelligence collection should ensure that monitoring is being done from the right sources. Simply conducting a Google search for the organization's name is not effective brand monitoring. There are companies, such as Recorded Future (www.recordedfuture.com)

and Cyveillance (www.cyveillance.com), that conduct primarily open source intelligence (OSINT), regarding brand monitoring as a subset of larger datasets, and can provide cyber security information specific to an organization.

Obviously, brand monitoring has other purposes within the organization. Marketing and product management teams often rely heavily on brand monitoring to ensure that their work aligns with the goals of the organization. As with the Governance, Risk Management, and Compliance (GRC) and Security Information and Event Management (SIEM) tools, there is no reason that a brand monitoring service cannot provide different information sets to different groups within the organization.

A cyber threat intelligence provider generally does not focus on finding information about a specific organization. There are a variety of threats that could hit an organization and the adversaries behind those threats do not publicly advertise their target list, assuming there is one to begin with. An exception to that rule, as hinted, is hacktivist attacks. *Hacktivist* is a term coined to describe a hacker cum activist. These are adversaries who have an axe to grind with whatever organization is being targeted and who wants that organization to know that it is being targeted and why. Hacktivists tend to broadcast their target information on Facebook or Twitter, or any place that will help them garner attention, and they love to chat with the press. Some hacktivists have access to botnets that are hundreds of thousands machines strong, and can cripple even the best prepared organizations. Other hacktivists are simply a guy in his mom's basement with an axe to grind.

This is a common misconception that many leaders have about the cyber threats facing their organization. The assumption is that the most severe attacks, the ones that are of the greatest concern to the organization, are targeted and completely customized for that organization. The majority of attacks, even sophisticated attacks, are more the result of chance than good planning by the adversary. An adversary may be targeting a specific sector, but that adversary is using the same infrastructure and the same tools across all attacks targeting that sector. When that adversary moves on to the next sector the adversary will continue to use the same toolset. Most attackers use what works and will continue to use it until it no longer works.

To this end, Tony Sager, chief technologist at Council on Cybersecurity, has three primary observations about cyber security (Jackson, 2010). The first is that, "The optimal place to solve a security problem is never where you found it." His second observation is, "If something is happening to you today, something identical or close to it happened to somebody yesterday and will happen to somebody else tomorrow." His final observation is "All the signs you needed to stop a threat or mitigate it were there, but they were not available to the cyber defender."

At its core, what Sager is describing is the problem of information sharing – far too often the people who need intelligence to protect their organization either don't have it, or don't notice it.

Are there exceptions to this rule? Absolutely. There are some organizations that are so secure and face such unique threats that elite groups using highly customized tools target them. Those organizations are few and far between, for most organizations an adversary will use the same tools to attack them that has been used on other targets.

That doesn't mean that those tools are not sophisticated and don't pose a serious threat. Adversaries are able to continuously reuse these tools precisely because they are powerful and difficult to detect. If attackers were using commodity malware to breach targets then the Firewall → Intrusion Detection System (IDS) → antivirus solution that so many organizations rely on would still be effective.

External intelligence gathering is about understanding these sophisticated tools and the actors behind them. It is also about understanding what the threats are today and what are the new threats. Tracking adversaries, their tactics, techniques, and procedures, and their infrastructure requires a great deal of access and specialized skills. Detecting adversaries who breach sophisticated organizations for a living without being detected is a skill in its own right.

This is why most organizations opt to purchase cyber threat intelligence rather than trying to collect it on their own. Simply speaking, the cost to set up an intelligence shop solely focused on monitoring and tracking existing threats is prohibitively expensive. It makes more sense to bring in that intelligence from one or more third parties and allow the security team to specialize in what they do best: protecting the organization.

ASSET, VULNERABILITY, AND CONFIGURATION MANAGEMENT

Now it's time to build on the work done in Chapter 5 (see p. 0000) by adding an intelligence overlay to the work. An intelligence overlay is really a pivot that allows an organization to correlate collected data against external data to produce an actionable event. Chapter 2 (see p. 0000) discussed the intelligence cycle; using that model, both internally collected data and intelligence feeds are collected into the same platform and then processed (correlated) looking for matches that better inform collected data and produce an actionable event during the analysis process.

In the realm of asset and vulnerability management that means being able to tie assets to known vulnerabilities using standards like Common Platform Enumeration (CPE) and Common Vulnerabilities and Exposures (CVE). Both of these standards fall under the realm of the Security Content Automation Protocol (SCAP) (scap.nist.gov).

SCAP combines a variety of existing standards that allow vendors to effectively communicate vulnerability information from one source to another. This allows a scanning tool to communicate scanning results to a GRC, which can also ingest a vulnerability data feed and tie both data sources together.

Figure 6.1 provides a good example of this, correlating information from multiple scanning sources into a single screen within LockPath's Keylight. In applying cyber threat intelligence to vulnerability data, the goal should always be to provide external context to the internal event. In effect, the external intelligence information should enhance the ability of the security team to properly rate the criticality of the vulnerability and decide on a course of action for dealing with that vulnerability.

Figure 6.2 shows the typical output of a Nessus (www.tenable.com) scan, it provides some detail around the vulnerabilities associated with the scanned host. It also provides (offscreen) a link to the CVE associated with this vulnerability, CVE-2011-3188.

Feeding the CVE information to an intelligence partner will provide a matching report that provides additional context around the nature of the threat, as shown in Figure 6.3. The Nessus scan provided information that there was a potential vulnerability

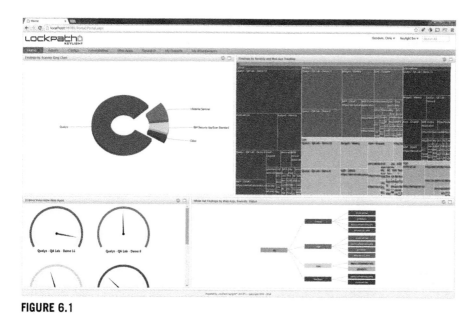

FIGURE 6.1

Correlating information from multiple scanning sources in LockPath.

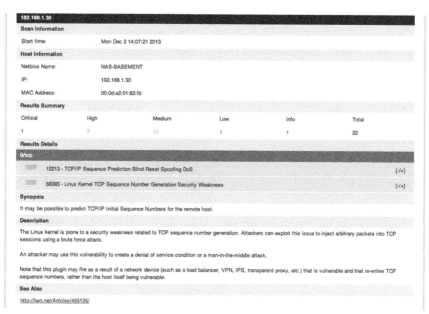

FIGURE 6.2

Sample output of a tenable Nessus scan.

Linux Kernel 2.6.39.4 TCP SeqNum Partial MD4 Insufficient Entropy Vulnerability

ThreatScape Vulnerability and Exploitation
March 11, 2014 18:00:25 PM CST, LOW, 11-16408, Version: [20]

Executive Summary
An insufficient entropy vulnerability exists in the use of partial MD4 for TCP sequence number generation in Linux Kernel 2.6.39.4 and earlier that, when exploited, allows an attacker to remotely bypass security restrictions. Exploit code is not publicly available.

Overview
An insufficient entropy vulnerability exists in the use of partial MD4 for TCP sequence number generation in Linux Kernel 2.6.39.4 and earlier that, when exploited, allows an attacker to remotely bypass security restrictions. Exploit code is not publicly available. Mitigation options include a vendor fix.

iSIGHT Partners considers this a Low-risk vulnerability due to the local network access and brute force needed to exploit this issue. Customers with specific questions regarding this vulnerability can contact the Vulnerability Research Team (VRT) at analystaccess@isightpartners.com.

FIGURE 6.3

Sample vulnerability report data surrounding CVE-2011-3188.

while the report from iSIGHT Partners[1] (www.isightpartners.com) provides additional context around that vulnerability. However, for these two datasets to turn into finished intelligence (FINTEL), the third piece is needed: the context around the vulnerable system.

This leads back to collecting both datasets into the GRC platform along with the network context provided by the system owner. Using the GRC as both the collection and processing platforms a security analyst can review both what is known about the vulnerability and what is known about the system and make a judgment with regard to the criticality level of patching. Fortunately, most intelligence providers make the job of correlating vulnerability data by providing vulnerability information via an Application Programming Interface (API), which translates vulnerability reporting information into a standard language that can be read by other machines:

```
<title><![CDATA[Linux Kernel 2.6.39.4 TCP SeqNum Partial
MD4 Insufficient Entropy Vulnerability]]></title>
<accessComplexity>AC:L</accessComplexity>
<accessVector>AV:A</accessVector>
<execSummary><![CDATA[An insufficient entropy
vulnerability exists in the use of partial MD4 for TCP
sequence number generation in Linux Kernel 2.6.39.4 and
earlier that, when exploited, allows an attacker to
remotely bypass security restrictions. Exploit code is
not publicly available.]]></execSummary>
<attackingEase>Difficult</attackingEase>
<authentication>Au:N</authentication>
<availabilityImpact>A:N</availabilityImpact> <bugTraqIds>
<bugTraqId>49289</bugTraqId> </bugTraqIds> <ThreatScape>
<product><![CDATA[ThreatScape Vulnerability and
Exploitation]]></product> </ThreatScape>
<confidentialityImpact>C:P</confidentialityImpact>
<cveIds> <cveId>CVE-2011-3188</cveId> </cveIds>
```

---

[1]In the interest of full-disclosure the author is an employee of iSIGHT Partners.

Programmatically integrating asset discovery data with external vulnerability intelligence data allows for the correlation to be done automatically. This brings the conversation back to SCAP. SCAP enables that programmatic union of datasets by tying them together along three different types of enumeration: Common Configuration Enumeration (CCE), CPE, and CVE. In addition to common enumerations, SCAP also provides for common risk scoring methodology using the Common Vulnerability Scoring System (CVSS). CVSS is critical to building FINTEL from vulnerability data. When the vulnerability is first released with a CVE number, it will have a CVSS score. When a vulnerability intelligence provider does its analysis it may assign the vulnerability a different CVSS score based on information about underground activity surrounding the vulnerability. A security analyst can take both scores into account, as well as the context of the vulnerable system to assign a third, and final, CVSS score based on the risk that system poses to the rest of the organization.

SCAP also uses a number of different languages to standardize the description of vulnerability information. Those languages are The eXtensible Configuration Checklist Description Format (XCCDF), Open Vulnerability and Assessment Language (OVAL), and Open Checklist Interactive Language (OCIL). More information about these languages is available on the National Institute of Standards and Technology (NIST) SCAP Web site (scap.nist.gov).

Most security vendors support at least some subset of the SCAP specifications; the most commonly supported are CPE, CVE, and CVSS. The CPE and CVE specifications are especially useful for connecting assets to vulnerabilities to exploitations. Connecting the dots in this way significantly improves the situational awareness of the security teams by tying the local system not just to a vulnerability but also to the exploit being used against that vulnerability. This often involves coordinating data from multiple sources. For example, look at CVE-2014-3936; below is a snippet (most of the alert has been snipped; this is simply for demonstration purposes) of the alert from the NIST National Vulnerability Database (nvd.nist.gov). The National Vulnerability Database provides vulnerability data feeds that can be downloaded and integrated into security products.

```
< entry id="CVE-2014-3936">
<vuln:references reference_type="UNKNOWN" xml:lang="en">
    <vuln:source>SECUNIA</vuln:source>
    <vuln:reference
href="http://secunia.com/advisories/58972"
xml:lang="en">58972</vuln:reference>
  </vuln:references>
  <vuln:references reference_type="UNKNOWN"
xml:lang="en">
    <vuln:source>SECUNIA</vuln:source>
    <vuln:reference
href="http://secunia.com/advisories/58728"
```

```
xml:lang="en">58728</vuln:reference>
   </vuln:references>
   <vuln:summary>Stack-based buffer overflow in the
do_hnap function in www/my_cgi.cgi in D-Link DSP-W215
(Rev. A1) with firmware 1.01b06 and earlier, DIR-505 with
firmware before 1.08b10, and DIR-505L with firmware 1.01
and earlier allows remote attackers to execute arbitrary
code via a long Content-Length header in a
GetDeviceSettings action in an HNAP
request.</vuln:summary>
   </entry>
```

Now, using the CVE number, a security analyst can check the vulnerability against exploits operating in the wild using a tool like Exploit Database (www. exploit-db.com – *warning:* some security tools block this as a malicious site) as shown in Figure 6.4.

Aside from the National Vulnerability Database, there are a number of vendors, such as Verisign's iDefense (www.verisigninc.com) and Symantec's DeepSight

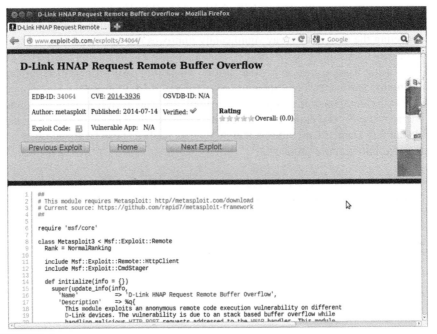

FIGURE 6.4

Exploit-DB output of exploits used against CVE-2014-3936.

(www.symantec.com), that provide vulnerability and exploitation information. With varying degrees of success, these vendors will also try to tie exploitation information to the vulnerability information. This affords a security analyst some insight into the operational and tactical threats against a particular vulnerability. By connecting the vulnerability to an exploit and understanding the nature of that exploit an analyst can now produce a customized CVSS score passed on the type of vulnerability, the ease of exploitation and the criticality of the vulnerable system to that network.

Alternatively, this method of collection and correlation provides the information necessary to plug the numbers into the Open Web Application Security Project (OWASP) equation: Risk = Likelihood * Impact. By collecting asset information, the security team has the data necessary to determine the impact to the organization if the vulnerable system is breached. Add to that the external cyber threat intelligence surrounding the vulnerability and the security team now has an idea of the likelihood of a security breach occurring. There are even ways to score the likelihood of a successful exploitation. Proof of concept exploit code does not present as high of a risk as a Metasploit module being created.

Whichever risk rating methodology is used having both the internal and external views of the threat will make it easier to apply a risk rating that is organization-specific and will allow the security team to better prioritize patching across the network.

At this point the only bit of missing data is information that will provide strategic intelligence. For the most part, strategic intelligence is not widely applied to vulnerability data. Simply put, once proof-of-concept code is released it becomes open season on a vulnerability and there will be wide range of adversaries attempting to exploit the vulnerability, especially if it is against a system or application that is widely deployed. Once a Metasploit module is developed, the number of attackers increases exponentially. Given this state of affairs, most organizations do not consider it worthwhile to tie an exploit to an individual or group, without additional corroborating information (discussed in the next sections).

That situation changes when the discussion revolves around so-called zero-day exploits. A zero-day exploit is one that takes advantage of a previously unknown, or at least unpublished, vulnerability in an application or system. The anatomy of the attack remains the same, but protecting against these types of attacks is more difficult, and there is usually a sophisticated adversary behind these attacks. There are more details on protecting against these attacks in a later section.

NETWORK LOGGING

Asset and configuration management rely heavily on standards like CPE and CVE to create pivot points to bring in external threat intelligence. As a component of security, network logging includes its own indicators that can act as pivot points to external cyber threat intelligence.

Sun Tzu said, "The rising of the birds in their flight is the sign of an ambuscade. Startled beasts indicate that a sudden attack is coming." Sun Tzu was referring to indicators of an attack, which are still one of the most effective methods of detecting an attack on an organization. Even though security teams cannot rely on birds or beasts as indicator sets,[2] there are a number of indicators within the organization that can be correlated against external cyber intelligence data to uncover threats against the organization.

If vulnerability intelligence is the first foray into intelligence for many organizations, indicator-based intelligence is usually the next step. Generally, indicator-based intelligence includes IP addresses, domains, URLs, and file hashes. There are a number of other indicators, some of which are discussed in later sections of this chapter, but these four are the primary sources of indicator-based intelligence.

How these data sources are brought in depends heavily on the source of the data, as well as the format of delivery. Some indicators are delivered simply as full reporting while others are delivered feeds that are designed to be simple black lists, still others are portal-based that require an analyst to manually examine suspicious indicators.

The fact is there are a variety of sources of indicator-based cyber threat intelligence. There are so much data that it can be confusing as to what sources to ingest and how to ingest that data.

Generally speaking, it is important to have a variety of threat intelligence sources that can be correlated against sources in the network. Different threat-intelligence providers have different insights into malicious activity occurring on, and off, the Internet. Some providers rely heavily on surface attack data to produce cyber threat intelligence. These providers generally have a large install base of security or networking tools and can collect data directly from their customers, anonymize it, and deliver it as threat intelligence based on real attack data. Blue Coat (www.bluecoat.com), McAfee (www.mcafee.com), and Symantec (www.symantec.com) are examples of companies that can provide this type of intelligence data. Other intelligence providers rely heavily on network monitoring to understand attack data. These providers have access to monitoring tools that sit directly on the largest Internet backbones or in the busiest data centers, so they are able to see a wide range of attack data as it flows from source to destination. Norse (www.norse-corp.com), Verisign (www.verisigninc.com), and Verizon (www.verizon.com) are examples of these types of providers. Then there are those intelligence providers that focus on the adversary. These providers track what different attack groups are doing and closely monitor their campaigns and infrastructure. This type of intelligence can be invaluable because adversary-focused intelligence can be proactive, knowing a group is about to launch an attack allows their customers to prepare before the attacks are launched. Examples of this type of provider include CrowdStrike (www.crowdstrike.com), iSIGHT Partners (www.isightpartners.com) and Mandiant (www.mandiant.com).

The above list is by no means exhaustive. Instead, it is meant to serve as a representative sample of the different types of intelligence providers out there and it is designed to help organizations ask the right questions when choosing an intelligence provider.

---

[2]Though, a carrier pigeon–based DDoS is an interesting attack vector.

There are also a number of excellent open source intelligence providers.[3] These providers generally rely on crowd-sourced intelligence. Crowd-sourced intelligence is a powerful tool because it allows for input from users all over the world; this creates a larger research organization than any one organization can produce. When done right, crowd-sourced open source cyber threat intelligence can be an invaluable asset to an organization. Unfortunately, when done wrong, it can generate large numbers of false-positives and produce mostly junk data. Some of the best open source threat intelligence data feeds include Abuse.ch (www.abuse.ch), Blocklist.de (www.blocklist.de), Emerging Threats (www.emergingthreats.net), and Spamhaus (www.spamhaus.org). The best open source cyber threat intelligence projects focus on a single type of threat or family of malware. This focus allows the teams behind the project to concentrate their efforts and produce the most accurate data for their users.

Again, by bringing in cyber threat intelligence data from a variety of sources an organization can benefit from the different views of malicious activity that each provider offers. Correlating intelligence from different organizations against data collected from inside the organization provides the security analyst with the external context surrounding the threat. Combining that external context with data collected internally allows a security analyst to accurately assess the threat and make recommendations for action commensurate with the specific threat to the organization.

IP ADDRESSES AS PIVOT POINTS

IP addresses are one of the most common pivot points used in intelligence analysis for defenders and victims. For security companies, it is typically a capability-based analysis model versus infrastructure-based model, given the exposure and volume of information collected. IP addresses are a great pivot point because they are ubiquitous across the network. Every system in the network communicates using IP addresses and, if the logs are being delivered to the SIEM, they present an easy pivot point that can be tracked across the network. Many intelligence providers provide out-of-the-box integrations into popular SIEMs, as well as other security tools. Even if out of the box integration is not available it is usually relatively trivial to get the data from the provider into the SIEM.

Figure 6.5 shows an example of intelligence delivered from CrowdStrike into a SIEM, it provides an IP address as well as other indicators all associated with a specific campaign. Pivoting off the IP address 1.9.5.38, a security analyst can link to full report (shown in Figure 6.6) to understand the nature of the threat that the adversary group Deep Panda poses to their organization.

In addition to the IP address, the threat intelligence feed also includes domains and file hashes associated with this particular adversary. Having this additional context allows a security analyst to engage in two different activities that security professionals are very familiar with: "blocking and tackling." Knowing that one indicator

---

[3]In this case, open source intelligence (OSINT), refers to open source as in open source software. OSINT is discussed later in this section.

```
{
  "success": true,
  "results": {
    "match": [
      {
        "feed_date": "2013-08-30",
        "feed_indicator": "1.9.5.38",
        "feed_type": "ip_address",
        "feed_actor": "DEEPPANDA",
        "feed_report": "CSIR-12000",
        "feed_domain_type": "",
        "feed_parse_type": "1"
      },
      {
        "feed_date": "2013-08-30",
        "feed_indicator": "47619fca20895abc83807321cbb80a3d",
        "feed_type": "hash_md5",
        "feed_actor": "DEEPPANDA",
        "feed_report": "CSIR-12000",
        "feed_domain_type": "",
        "feed_parse_type": "1"
      },
      {
        "feed_date": "2013-08-30",
        "feed_indicator": "infoctrs.dll",
        "feed_type": "file_name",
        "feed_actor": "DEEPPANDA",
        "feed_report": "CSIR-12000",
        "feed_domain_type": "",
        "feed_parse_type": "1"
      },
      {
        "feed_date": "2013-08-30",
        "feed_indicator": "de7500fc1065a081180841f32f06a517",
        "feed_type": "hash_md5",
        "feed_actor": "DEEPPANDA",
        "feed_report": "CSIR-12000",
        "feed_domain_type": "",
        "feed_parse_type": "1"
      },
      {
        "feed_date": "2013-08-30",
        "feed_indicator": "14c04f88dc97aef3e9b516ef208a2bf5",
        "feed_type": "hash_md5",
        "feed_actor": "DEEPPANDA",
        "feed_report": "CSIR-12000",
        "feed_domain_type": "",
        "feed_parse_type": "1"
      },
      {
        "feed_date": "2013-08-30",
        "feed_indicator": "infoadmn.dll",
        "feed_type": "file_name",
        "feed_actor": "DEEPPANDA",
        "feed_report": "CSIR-12000",
        "feed_domain_type": "",
        "feed_parse_type": "1"
```

FIGURE 6.5

Sample of CrowdStrike IP address-based intelligence.

associated with this adversary is in the network, there is a good chance the others may be present, so a security analyst can begin querying other systems looking for those artifacts, whether they are file hashes, other IP addresses, or domains. If the needed data is not already collected within the SIEM, the security analyst can work with the incident response team to look for those indicators.

If, as often is the case, the security analyst is also part of the incident response team, the security analyst can load the new set of indicators into the incident response tool and track down the indicators across the network, tackling them before they can do further damage. While the tackling of existing indicators is being done, a second report can be sent to the team who manages the edge security devices to block the other indicators associated with this threat.

This is a great example, of using intelligence to react to attacks that exist within the network. But this type of intelligence can also be used to proactively defend the organization. Stopping attacks before they have a chance to pose a serious threat to

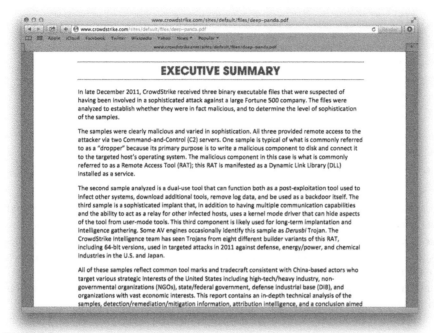

FIGURE 6.6

The link to the full CrowdStrike report.

the organization is a prime example of predictive, intelligence-led security. The ZeuS tracker block list hosted by Abuse.ch is an example of this type of predictive security. The list is a simple list, updated daily that provides the most recent ZeuS nodes (this is just a sample of the list):

```
################################################################
#                                                              #
# abuse.ch ZeuS IP blocklist "BadIPs" (excluding hijacked      #
#                                                              #
# sites and free hosting providers)                            #
#                                                              #
#                                                              #
#                                                              #
# For questions please refer to                                #
#                                                              #
# https://zeustracker.abuse.ch/blocklist.php                   #
#                                                              #
################################################################


103.230.84.239
103.24.3.198
103.241.0.100
103.4.52.150
```

```
103.7.59.135
107.150.58.84
107.181.174.84
108.166.181.239
108.175.149.16
108.61.123.204
108.61.208.120
108.61.210.194
108.61.252.184
108.61.63.78
109.120.150.246
109.120.183.106
109.127.8.242
109.229.210.250
```

Note that Abuse.ch has already removed both redirect and free hosting providers from the list, which significantly cuts down on the false-positives and provides a greater level of confidence in the provided data. Correlating this information against logs collected within the network should allow security analysts to better determine if there is a new variant of ZeuS in their network, and if there isn't a new variant, block any attempts to reach the ZeuS command-and-control infrastructure from within the organization.

Although IP addresses are a great pivot point because of their ubiquity and the amount of sources available to check against, there is one major problem with using IP addresses as a pivot point: a high rate of false-positives. The time to live (TTL) for an IP address as an effective indicator of compromise can be very low. Compromised hosts get patched, illicitly acquired hosting space is turned off, and malicious hosts are quickly identified and blocked or the traffic is black-holed by the ISP. Even when an IP address is being used for malicious activity it can sometimes be hard to block. Blocking an IP address on a shared hosting server with thousands of other legitimate sites, means also blocking all of those sites.

IP addresses are very valuable pivot points, but security teams must be conscious of the short TTL and take that into account when taking action against an IP address. Many intelligence providers include a TTL along with the indicators they provide. For providers that do not include TTLs, each organization that subscribes to their intelligence needs to determine the TTL they are going to set for each type of indicator. An IP address may have a TTL of two weeks, while domains and file hashes would have significantly longer TTLs.

DOMAIN NAMES AS PIVOT POINTS

Domain names make an interesting pivot point because they can be used to track down more information about an adversary than an IP address can. Domain names also have a longer TTL – often a domain name that is being used for malicious activity remains malicious for its entire registration existence (though not always). Finally, domain names have more blocking points within the organization. A security analyst can stop a domain at the edge by including it in the firewall, mail filter, or proxy, or the analyst can stop the domain at the core of the network by adding it to a black hole on the Domain Name System (DNS) server.

As demonstrated with the DNS tunneling example in Chapter 5 (see p. 0000), there is a great deal of intelligence that can be produced internally around a domain name. Sometimes, this can make it a more effective pivot point than an IP address, because the security analyst knows the collected information is specific and relevant to the analyst's organization.

There is a great deal of potential OSINT around a domain just using basic domain lookup tools. DNS research can be a powerful tool in the hands of a well-trained security analyst.

Take the example highlighted in Figures 6.7 and 6.8. An analyst uncovers a suspicious domain TrendMicro-Update.org on the SIEM. Maybe the domain hit a threshold of too many callouts in a short period of time, or maybe the traffic was malformed for the protocol it was using. For whatever reason, the analyst flagged the domain and went to the DomainTools Web site (www.domaintools.com) to look up the domain. The domain is clearly not registered to anyone associated with Trend Micro, which raises suspicions.

But more interesting is the link to other domains associated with the email address of the registrant. As shown in Figure 6.8, those other domains are google-analytics. com, and microsoftinforms.com. The fact that the registrant is coopting the names of the three companies to make the traffic appear more legitimate confirms that the original domain is most likely malicious. However, in addition to that, the analyst can now add the other two domains to the block list, and ensure that there is no traffic

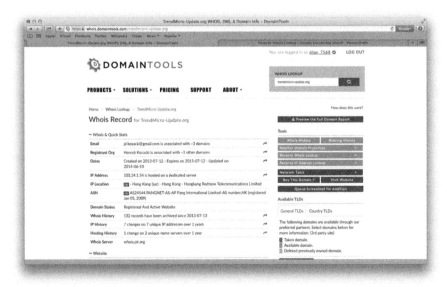

FIGURE 6.7

DomainTools lookup of domain TrendMicro-Update.org.

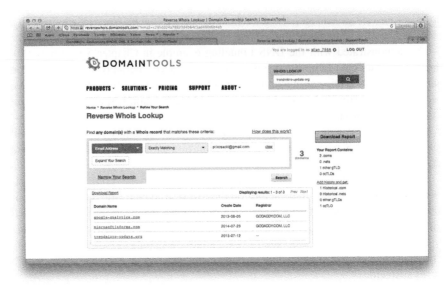

FIGURE 6.8

Other domains registered by the same user.

flowing from the network to those domains. As an additional security step, the analyst can set an alert for whenever that email is associated with a new domain registration. Now, the security analyst has the ability to proactively block new domains from that adversary before they can be used to do damage to the organization (as long as the adversary continues to use the same email address to register domains).

Another great source of OSINT is Recorded Future (www.recordedfuture.com). Recorded Future can provide graphic displays of information around a domain being used maliciously. For example, a security analyst discovers the suspect domain weatheronline.hopto.org. By using the Record Future console, the security analyst can see if the domain has been associated with malicious OSINT reporting (Figure 6.9).

The analyst can expand the search to the entire hopto.org domain, which shows a large amount of malicious activity associated with the entire domain, as shown in Figure 6.10.

Clearly, there are a large number of malicious domains associated with hopto.org. Now the organization has to decide whether or not the domain poses a threat to the organization and whether or not it should be completely blocked.

One way to do that is to switch from OSINT to other sources of intelligence to understand more about the threat the adversary behind this domain poses. A query on the iSIGHT Partners portal, shown in Figure 6.11, reveals that there are several other domains associated with this particular threat and there are also a number of IP addresses and file hashes. The report also discusses the tactics, techniques, and procedures (TTPs) of this particular actor, which the security analyst can now use to enhance security measures within the organization while the additional indicators can be hunted for throughout the network.

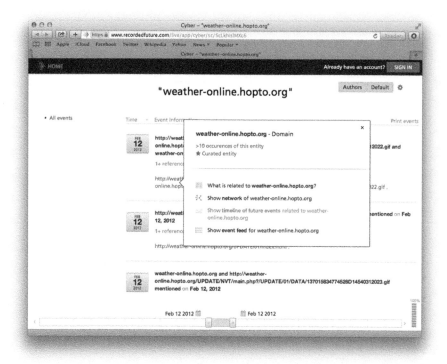

FIGURE 6.9

OSINT references to weather-online.hopto.org in Recorded Future.

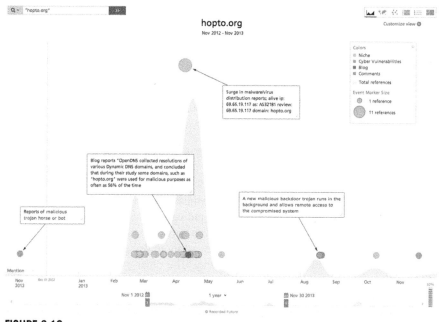

FIGURE 6.10

Recorded Future mapping OSINT references to hopto.org.

Threat Detail

Uroburos and Relationship to Agent.btz

Defense Contractors and U.S. Government (Intel-1234661)

ThreatScape Products

Cyber Espionage

Open-source reporting released in late February 2014 indicates the discovery of an advanced rootkit known as "Uroburos" named for a string found in the malware's code. Uroburos is modular malware that can grant control of an infected machine, execute arbitrary commands, hide system activities and capture network traffic and exfiltrate data.

Following preliminary analysis of the malware, iSIGHT Partners agrees that Uroburos is closely tied to a worm dubbed Agent.btz, malware highly publicized in 2008 as a complex threat impacting systems and networks associated with the U.S. Government. The following points suggest a relationship between Uroburos and Agent.btz:

- Uroburos checks for the presence of Agent.btz following successful compromise possibly indicating the actors behind Uroburos campaigns are monitoring systems infected with either malware.
- Both pieces of malware use the obfuscation key 1dM3uu4j7Fw4sjnbcwlDqet4m5Imnxl1pz xl6as80cbLnmz54cs5Ldn4ri3do5L6gs923HL34x2f5cvd0fk6c1a0s
- Uroburos and Agent.btz use winview.ocx to store logs.

Infection Vector

Although, the exact manner in which Uroburos infects victim hosts is unknown, there are a variety of methods through which the malware can be transmitted. As was the case with Agent.btz, the malware can be transferred to victims' systems via infected USB drive. In addition, targeted e-mail campaigns, watering hole or drive-by infections, are among conceivable exploitation methods.

Network Infrastructure

As we are continuing to analyze and process data associated with Uroburos, the extent of the malware's command and control (C&C) infrastructure is unclear. However, information acquired via a sensitive source that has not yet been independently verified indicates the following domains are associated with the family of malware including Uroburos and Agent.btz:

IP Address	Domain
82.141.230.146	academyawards.effers.com
62.65.252.15	allnews.ath.cx
80.246.199.24	allnews.ath.cx
198.199.78.132	arctic-zone.bbsindex.com
124.248.207.50	arctic-zone.bbsindex.com
59.125.160.178	biznews.ath.cx
80.246.199.24	biznews.podzone.org
80.246.199.24	breakingnews.ath.cx
124.248.207.50	cars-online.zapto.org

FIGURE 6.11

Adversarial intelligence from iSIGHT Partners.

Of course, hopping from portal to portal in this manner can be exhausting and slow down the ability of the security analysts to respond to other security events. Which is why it is better, whenever possible to bring, the data directly into the platform the analysts are using. Each of the providers discussed so far has either an API or a static Web site where they publish indicators or full reports. Using the API or writing a scraping tool that automates the process of loading data from the intelligence provider into the SIEM and other security tools improves the efficiency of the collection and processing processes. These steps also help lessen the likelihood that something will be missed during the analysis process.

FILE HASHES AS PIVOT POINTS

File hashes are the least used but potentially the most powerful pivot point within cyber threat intelligence. File hashes have the longest TTL and it is very unlikely that a file hash will return a false-positive. File hashes provide security analysts with an immediate resolution as to whether or not an indicator is bad.

But there are very few security tools, or even network systems in general that will allow a security team to pivot off file hashes, so monitoring for suspicious activity on the network using file hashes can be tricky. The other challenge is that making changes to a program changes its hash, meaning that an organization can quickly amass a large quantity of file hashes that continuously need to be updated. Of course, the same problem is true about IP addresses and domains. The trick is to properly manage these lists, dropping off entries that are no longer relevant while adding in new entries in a timely fashion. Incorporating black/white list maintenance into the intelligence cycle of an organization improves the efficiency of the security team and can also improve the efficiency of the network systems by ensuring that the systems are not weighed down with old and irrelevant entries.

One rather unique aspect of using file hashes as a pivot point is the ability to use file hash white lists as an effective security tool. White lists are lists of item that are acceptable. So, rather than blocking things that are bad, a white list starts with the assumption that everything is bad and that only the things on this list are good. White lists used to be common in Web proxies, when the Internet was a lot smaller. The problem with a white list in a modern organization is that it quickly grows untenable as users of the network have different business (and, to be honest, nonbusiness) reasons to visit a large number of domains.

Unlike, IP address and domain names, a properly deployed file hash white list can make a lot of sense. It is unrealistic to maintain a white list of every file in organization. Some files, like Word Documents, PDF files, Excel spreadsheets, and database tables are constantly changing.

On the other hand, the files that comprise the operating systems in use throughout the network are relatively static, as are the files that are part of approved applications in use on the network. So, although a Microsoft Word file may be constantly changing, Microsoft Word itself does not. This goes back to the idea of using asset management tools to monitor changes to desktop applications discussed in Chapter 5 (see p. 0000). The difference in this case is that instead of direct application monitoring, the organization is monitoring for anything that is not allowed.

For this to work, the organization first has to have a standardized desktop installation as well as a list of approved applications. Anything outside of the approved applications has to go through a well-defined approval process that includes hashing the files associated with the application.

Once that is in place, there are several different ways to proceed. One way is to create hashes of all the files in the operating system and program directories. Any time a change is made to any of those files an alert is sent and the security team can respond. The problem with this method is that adversaries get around it by installing their executable files in temp directories, or other areas that are often not closely monitored. The alternative is to simply create hashes of all the allowed executable files within the organization. Agents such as Bit9 (www. bit9.com) or Symantec's Critical System Protection (www.symantec.com) feed directly into the SIEM, and generate an alert that the security analyst can investigate whenever a file that does not match an existing file hash executes anywhere on the system.

Internally, this file is known to be suspect but right now there is no additional information surrounding the file. An analyst has to determine if there is anything else known about the file and unless the organization has a malware lab (more on this in Chapter 9) that involves reaching out to external sources.

Two of the most commonly used tools for online file submission are VirusTotal (www.virustotal.com) and ThreatExpert (www.threatexpert.com). Both services allow users to search their database for file hashes that have already been submitted and they allow users to submit malware samples for review and will provide reports back on those submissions. The difference is that VirusTotal provides information about what different antivirus vendors know about a particular file hash, whereas ThreatExpert provides a report breaking down the actions of the executable. Both sources provide a great deal of contextual information about the "goodness or badness" of a file, as shown in Figure 6.12. VirusTotal and ThreatExpert both also have an API that allows file hashes to be queried programmatically, rather than having to visit a portal.

In addition to submitting to these OSINT tools, the file (or file hash) can also be submitted to an intelligence provider to see if they can return any adversary information on the attack. At the very least they should be able to return any IP addresses and domains associated with the hash.

Many security vendors also offer file analysis services at no additional charge. The time to find out about these services and, most importantly, the service level agreements associated with them, is before there is a suspicious file uncovered within the organization. Knowing that a file analysis can be turned around quickly gives the

FIGURE 6.12

Results of hash lookup in VirusTotal.

eSentire has detected a Malware Download from this machine.
[US Federal Agency/CERT incident Category: CAT 3]

This does not necessarily mean that the malware has infected the machine - merely that we have detected that the code transfer was effected by the system (either inadvertently - through an embedded link, or by a specific request by the user).

Please open a Priority 3 Ticket for desktop technicians to investigate the situation.

We recommend:
a) A manual Anti-Virus scan be performed
b) A manual Anti-Malware scan be performed (using at least one tool)
c) Anti-Virus signatures are verified to be up-to-date
d) The user be queried about their activity during this time (to determine whether or not they intentionally downloaded the software in question)

Local IP Address:	10.100.10.222
Local Hostname:	APRABSHAKAR
Malware Detected:	Fake Java Update
Download Source:	hxxp:/ /www[dot]istplayer[dot]com/entry/node/file/pkg/loader/java_installer[dot]exe?offer_id=13232[and]aff_id=20749[and]transaction_id=ef814f19-ab58-4eff-a262-0f8c9f954e6d
Remote IP Address:	54.183.112.80
Malicous File:	java_installer.exe

Please let us know if you would like us to implement a TCP block between this external IP and your internal network.

Also, please acknowledge receipt of this alert.

FIGURE 6.13

An eSentire malware blocking alert.

security team peace of mind that they will be able to respond in a timely manner to a security incident involving an unknown file.

PIVOTING FROM MSSP ALERTS

Alerts from a Managed Security Services Provider (MSSP) can also make excellent pivot points to tie an activity to an actor or group. While most MSSP have good attack surface data, they don't always have a lot of information tied to the adversaries behind the attacks on their customers.

Take, for example, the eSentire alert in Figure 6.13. The MSSP does a good job of tying the operational and tactical threats together by correlating the malicious domain with the malware being used by the adversary. By feeding that information into the organization's intelligence cycle, preferably programmatically, of course, the alert from the MSSP can help flesh out the information the organization has about the adversary. An MSSP alert may augment existing intelligence, or it may provide an entirely new insight into an adversary, as long as it is integrated as part of the intelligence cycle.

NETWORK MONITORING

A lot of the same principles described in the previous section also apply to live network monitoring. Real-time monitoring tools are designed to monitor for specific traffic patterns that are indicative of malicious activity. However, using the programmatic interfaces available on these platforms organizations can bring in third-party intelligence to be much more proactive in stopping attacks. Figure 6.14 is an example of how intelligence can enhance the security capabilities of these platforms.

Depending on the network monitoring tool in place, the addition of intelligence can allow an attack to be stopped before it has a chance to be successful. This is an area where file hashes, in particular, are a useful addition. Identifying a malicious file

FIGURE 6.14

Adding intelligence information to Reservoir's R-Scope platform.

in transit and alerting on it means an intelligence-led security team can get to the target machine before the file is successfully installed, or at least before it has a chance to exfiltrate data from the organization.

There are a number of enterprising developers who have written scripts that bring in data from VirusTotal and other OSINT platforms directly into heuristic network security monitors, such as Bro (www.bro.org). Using these tools can capture a lot of valuable data at the network level.

YARA

YARA (plusvic.github.io/yara) is an open-source tool used to create free-form signatures that can be used to tie indicators to actors. Those signatures can be integrated across multiple platforms within the network, including a variety of network monitoring tools.

YARA is a perfect example of the next generation of intelligence tools. Cyber intelligence, today, is mostly focused around indicators. Indicators are not intelligence. Indicators connect network activity happening within the organization to adversarial activity happening outside of the organization. That connection is what produced true cyber threat intelligence.

Because YARA focuses on pattern matching, it opens up the ability of the security analyst to create signatures outside of the traditional indicator box that contains only IP addresses, domains, and file hashes. Although these are all valuable indicators and can be used within YARA, there are other types of indicators that are harder to map, which YARA's extensibility is able to support. There is a reason it is called the "Swiss Army Knife of malware research." A typical YARA signature looks like this:

```
rule Koala Team {
    meta:
        description = "C&C Activity Associated with Koala"
strings:
        $a = "10bestsearch.com"
        $b = "XAML"
        $c = "B6"
    condition:
     $a or ($b and $c)   }
```

The above signature uses elements associated with KOALA Team and combines them into a single signature. The signature includes a known malicious domain that KOALA Team uses, 10bestsearch.com, but it also includes known commands issued by the command-and-control infrastructure: XAML and B6. The rule tells the security system to issue an alert whenever that domain is seen in the network, or if it sees both XAML and B6 in network traffic.

Adversaries jump very quickly from one domain to another. They do this so often that it can be a challenge to keep up with them. However, command-and-control infrastructure is relatively stagnant, so including these two commands enables systems to alert on activity associated with KOALA even if KOALA are using a previously unseen domain.

The other advantage to the YARA signatures is that, as in the example above, they can be associated with the adversary as opposed to just the malware family. As additional information associated with this adversary is gathered from various sources it can be combined into a single signature or multiple signatures all tied to the group.

This section has provided a very high level overview of YARA, it is definitely a tool worth investigating further.

PROTECTING AGAINST ZERO-DAY ATTACKS

Zero-day attacks pose a great concern to many organizations, especially to the security teams within those organizations. These security teams, who often cannot keep up with the known alerts, have no idea how to handle an unknown attack.

Chapter 3 discussed the Lockheed Martin Kill Chain model, which lists the various phases associated with an attack ranging from Reconnaissance through Exfiltration. Whether an adversary is a sophisticated attacker or a newbie they are going to follow roughly the same set of phases. Because of this universal methodology, there are several points in the attack processes where cyber threat intelligence can provide information that may stop the attack. There are also other steps an organization can take, based on past successful breaches within the organization to better improve the security of the organization.

Let's start with a fact that has been emphasized a few times throughout this book: Very rarely are zero-day attacks really zero-day. Just because an antivirus vendor does not have a signature for the malware or the domains the adversary are using have not made it to a block list yet, does not mean that the adversary hasn't used the same tools on another target. There are a lot of very insecure organizations around the around. Attack groups know this and the most sophisticated ones will often test tools by launching attacks against those low security targets, and tweaking their tools based on the result of those attacks.

A threat intelligence provider that is adversary focused, one that is monitoring activity of attack groups and is familiar with the TTPs of those groups, can use this information to provide predictive intelligence to their clients. Often released with titles similar to "Group X Preparing to Launch Attacks Against U.S. Targets" or "Group X Planning Campaign Against the Financial Industry," these types of reports give organizations the opportunity to be predictive in their intelligence. But for an organization to take advantage of that intelligence, it must be tracking campaigns internally.

For example, when Mandiant (www.mandiant.com) released its report on Comment Crew (Mandiant referred to them as APT1), it also released a wide range of indicators. Organizations were able to review logs to determine whether or not they were a victim of Comment Crew. If an organization was a victim of a Comment Crew intrusion, there is a good chance that it will be targeted again. So, when Mandiant, or any cyber intelligence threat provider, releases an update on Comment Crew activities that new information should be correlated against previous Comment Crew activities targeting the organization. The updated operational and tactical intelligence combined with the strategic outlook, both external and internal, allow security analysts to produce FINTEL specific to the organization.

Comment Crew is a perfect example of how the "zero-day" attack is very rarely a zero-day attack. Comment Crew used the same tools across multiple organizations and sectors. Had there been better communication between organizations and better use of Information Sharing and Analysis Centers (ISACs – discussed in more detail in Chapter 8), Comment Crew may have become widely known, and blocked, sooner.

Unfortunately, there is not always advanced intelligence on such groups. Not that the same pattern doesn't play out, but it simply may not be observed. Even the best intelligence organizations cannot watch every part of the Internet for malicious activity. In those cases where intelligence cannot inform on the attack in advance, it is up to the security team to configure security systems to alert on patterns indicative of malicious activity.

Some of those patterns have already been discussed: monitoring for unusual user activity within the network – especially administrative users, monitoring for suspicious DNS traffic, monitoring for network traffic is that not compliant with the purported protocol that is being used, and looking for executable files in the wrong place or that are not on the white list.

Notice that each of these activities lines up well with different elements of the Lockheed Martin Kill Chain, but there are some additional things that can be done, using the same tools, that many organizations have not considered.

Both Bit9 and Critical System Protection can look for large files that suddenly appear in the temp or other directories where they should not. The last step in the Kill Chain model is exfiltration of collected data. To do that the data has to be collected somewhere before being moved off the network. This generally means large files in places where there should not normally be large files. Monitoring for large file creation, especially after normal work hours, and stopping the transfer before it can leave the network means stopping the adversary from achieving its goal.

Another way to detect previously unknown malicious behavior is to monitor for and block any poorly signed certificates of authority. This is along the lines of mal-formed protocol monitoring. More attackers are moving from HTTP and the protocol of choice to HTTPS. But it is surprisingly difficult for a group engaging in malicious activities to acquire an SSL certificate. This means these groups are often forced to use self-signed certificates or, worse, attempt to create fakes certificates in an at-tempt to look like Microsoft or Google. Although SSL traffic secured using a fake certificate is still encrypted, the certificate information is passed in the clear. Network monitoring tools can easily pick out a noncompliant certificate and alert that the traf-fic should be blocked.

Finally, monitoring for anomalous traffic is another way to stop a potential zero-day attack, though this means stopping it very late in the intrusion process; by then it may be too late. Looking for high levels of traffic from systems, especially desktops, after hours can be an indication that malicious data is leaving the network.[4] Unfor-tunately, stopping it at this point means that some core data has most likely left the network.

If an organization is a victim of a zero-day attack, it is important to collect as much information about the attack as possible. Make an image of any infected sys-tems before wiping them and collect as many relevant logs as possible. Using this information, security analysts can build a view of the attack, finding out the intru-sion point and determining which security systems failed and why. After piecing together the attack, especially if it is one that is unique, that information should be shared with trusted security partners as well as any industry groups. As much as be-ing compromised is painful, being able to protect other organizations in the same sec-tor means that everyone's security is improved. Hopefully, when those organizations are inevitably breached, they will do the same thing and this information sharing will continue across the sector.

INCIDENT RESPONSE AND INTELLIGENCE

One of the assumptions of the security frameworks discussed in earlier chapters, and an assumption made in every effective security framework, is that eventually an orga-nization is going to be breached. In fact, the assumption about using indicator-based

---

[4]It also could be a sign that Netflix has released the new season of "Orange is the New Black," which may be a different security problem.

intelligence is that the adversaries are going to find a way into the network; the goal then is to quickly isolate the breach and contain the damage to the organization.

The focus of the Chapters 4 and 5 has been on using security systems, with an intelligence overlay, to identify attacks on or within the network. It goes without saying that identifying the attacks is not enough; an intelligence-led security program must have an intelligence-led incident response team that is as nimble and proactive as the security team – the reality is that in many organizations the security team and the incident response team are one and the same.

Incident response teams can adopt the tactics used by security teams to fuse intelligence into their day-to-day activities. In many cases, the connecting nature of third-party cyber threat intelligence makes even more sense in an incident response environment.

Take CrowdStrike's Deep Panda example from earlier in this chapter. The API version of the report includes IP address 1.9.5.38 as well as the file name infoctrs.dll and the MD5 hash 47619fca20895abc83807321cbb80a3d. The security team may have alerted on one of these indicators, but knowing that they are all tied to the Deep Panda group, the incident response teams need to be able to quickly check all systems on the network for matches to all of the indicators.

That is where incident response tools such as Co3 Systems (www.co3sys.com) and Carbon Black (www.carbonblack.com) come into play. These systems allow an incident response team to load custom indicators directly into platform and automatically reach out to all machines in the network (those that have the agent installed) to look for matches (Figure 6.15).

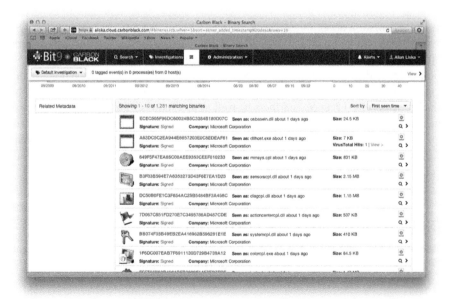

FIGURE 6.15

A Carbon Black match against VirusTotal indicators.

Both platforms also enable intelligence integration automatically using the APIs of supported vendors. This allows the incident response team to take advantage of multiple sources of intelligence simultaneously within a single platform, increasing the likelihood that multiple artifacts tied to an adversary will be uncovered during the investigation process.

Carbon Black eases the hunting for the artifacts by using an agent running on the desktops and servers within the organization that is collecting information about artifacts all the time. The Carbon Black agent also has a series of checks that it runs against applications on the desktop looking for potential malware. These checks are completely independent from the indicators being fed through the console by the incident response team.

Whatever tool an incident response team uses to investigate a potential breach adding cyber threat intelligence into that investigation will allow the investigator to understand all of the known artifacts associated with that actor or group. Tying the indicators together into the investigation process helps to ensure that important artifacts are not overlooked and that the threat is fully removed from the organization.

COLLABORATIVE RESEARCH INTO THREATS

Collaborative research into threats (CRITs) (crits.github.io) is an open source malware repository that relies on OSINT to manage and share indicator sets within and across organizations. CRITs uses emerging standards such as STIX, CyBOX, and TAXII to deliver threat information from one system to another in a standardized format (more on these standards in Chapter 7).

By tying artifacts to campaign information, CRITs creates pivot points that malware analysts and security teams can use to further investigate threats within their organization. CRITs also allows organizations to tag the data as they see fit; what one organization may tag as an artifact related to ZeuS, another might tag as related to CryptoLocker – each user has the ability to make those changes.

To create effective pivot points CRITs relies on 12 top-level objects (TLOs). Those 12 TLOs are: actors, campaigns, certificates, domains, emails, events, indicators, IPs, PCAPs, raw data, samples, and targets. Each of these TLOs is a pivot point within CRITs that can then be tied to other TLOs. These joined groups can then be sent to security teams for additional investigation or they can be tied together as a single campaign.

CRITs also has a built-in dashboard that allows the security analyst to easily visualize the relationship between these different TLOs. The dashboard also allows for easy sharing of information, as well as for pushing information to other platforms.

There is a lot of excitement in the security community surrounding CRITs and its ability to improve the efficiency of security teams as well as provide greater, crowd-sourced, insight into the threats that are facing multiple organizations.

CONCLUSION

This chapter touched on a lot of topics related to cyber threat intelligence within the security realm. Although there was a heavy emphasis on using indicators such as IP addresses, domains, and file hashes as pivot points, it is important to remember that indicators of compromise (IOCs) do not equate intelligence.

Cyber threat intelligence is really about providing information that is necessary for an organization to make an informed decision, true cyber threat intelligence is actionable. An IP address is not, in and of itself, intelligence; .it is the context that comes with the IP address that is true intelligence.

Cyber threat intelligence serves a role beyond the use in day-to-day security monitoring. Threat intelligence can also be an invaluable tool in incident response or when protecting the organization against zero-day attacks.

Finally, the field of cyber threat intelligence is a young one that is continuing to grow at a fast clip. That fast growth means there are a lot of exciting projects like CRITs and YARA that up and coming and worth getting to know.

REFERENCES

Jackson, W., 2010. Better cybersecurity depends on better information management. <http://gcn.com/Articles/2010/06/22/Information-management-better-cybersecurity.aspx>. (accessed 19.09.14.).

Tzu, S., The Art of War, (Lionel Giles, Trans.). Polity, New York, p. 31.

Fusing internal and external intelligence

7

- Security awareness training
- OpenIOC, CyBOX, STIX, and TAXII
- Threat intelligence management platforms
- Big data security analytics

INTRODUCTION

To this point the discussion has revolved around correlating and fusing intelligence into security systems inside the organization. But to take security to the next level and move toward Intelligence-Guided Computer and Network Defense (IGCND), the integration of intelligence into security systems has to be seamless.

The flow of both internal and external information into the collection and processing. While a good security analyst will weigh the value of collected data differently depending on the source, access to the actual data should ultimately be the same across all sources in use by the organization.

This is really the final step in becoming an intelligence-led organization. When data sources are fused together in such a way that indicators from multiple sources can easily be tied to adversary groups, and the analysts building FINTEL have access to contextual information about the quality of the incoming data so as to make better decisions as to how to use the data, then an intelligence organization is full intelligence-led.

In Chapters 5 and 6, the focus was on the Security Information and Event Management (SIEM) and Governance, Risk Management, and Compliance (GRC) as the integration points. There are a lot of advantages to the SIEM environment, but a SIEM treats all data sources equally. The SIEM relies on self-reporting from the source or correlation rules to determine the severity of an incident. Although the GRC environment is more flexible, it was not designed from the ground-up to operate within an intelligence cycle environment.

The focus of this chapter is fusing internal and external data in such a way that the data presents a single, focused picture of the threat to the organization.

SECURITY AWARENESS TRAINING

Awareness training may seem like a complete non sequitur based on the previous discussion, but it really isn't. Too many organizations do not engage in security awareness training for their users and customers. Those organizations that do often limit themselves to a high-level overview of the security reports such as the Verizon Data Breach Report (www.verizonenterprise.com) or the Symantec Internet Security Threat Report (www.symantec.com) Although these reports contain valuable information for the enterprise and are useful overall, they generally do not make for a good basis for security awareness training.

Good security awareness training should be relevant to the organization. It is one thing for users to know that clicking on links is bad; it is quite another thing to note that people within the organization have fallen victim to these specific attack campaigns. By highlighting not only the larger threat, but also the specific threat to the organization, users are more involved in the security process and are going to be more aware to potential threats.

As with monitoring, security awareness training needs to be a continuous process. Not only should users understand the latest threats, they should understand the impact their actions can have on the organization.

Security professionals sometimes forget that most users within the organization are not thinking about security all of the time. Continuous security awareness training helps to keep security always in the mind of the users. Network users can serve as an additional source of information included in an intelligence-led security program – in effect they can become assets.

In conjunction with the creation of the security awareness training, a method for users to report suspicious activity should also be created. Generally speaking, that method should not be an email address, it should be a web form or some other method that can be integrated into the established intelligence cycle. User reporting should be integrated into the intelligence cycle and be correlated against all of the other information being collected by the security team, making user reports another data stream that goes into the production of FINTEL.

Remember that the primary method of access into an organization is through the users. Finding new ways to get a user to click on a link or open a loaded document is an important part of the attack methodology for many adversaries. If network users are thinking about that when they receive an email from someone they don't know, or attending an event on behalf of the organization, they are much less likely to blindly click on links. They will also be more aware if they do click and something happens.

Users will also be more likely to inform the security team if something suspicious happens if they know the potential risk to the organization. As has been mentioned previously, even the best-defended networks are going to be breached, so having the users of the network act as extensions of the security team means that those breaches can be caught earlier.

All that being said, security training should not be scary. Yes, the weight of a security breach should be stressed, users need to know that security should be taken seriously, but fear has never been the most effective communication tool.

For instance, many organizations use cyber security posters like those found at Schweitzer Engineering Laboratories (www.selinc.com), an example of which is shown in Figure 7.1. These posters serve as a constant reminder of the importance of cyber security to the organization, using humor to attract the attention of users and, hopefully, to keep the thought in the back of the minds of the users.

Working with cyber threat intelligence partners to craft organization-specific training can be invaluable to users on the network. Some threat-intelligence providers, such as iSIGHT Partners (www.isightpartners.com) even provide materials such as their monthly "Potential Targeted Malware Infection Lures," shown in Figure 7.2. These tools take current known threats facing a variety of sectors and allow the security team to customize them based on what is being seen within the organization. This allows the training to be customized to the organization, but based on cyber threat intelligence regarding threats currently impacting other organizations.

Security awareness training does not have to be classroom based; it can be done via videoconference or even a monthly newsletter, although a videoconference is much more likely to be attended and paid attention to than an email that may sit unread until long after it is too late.

FIGURE 7.1

A Schweitzer Engineering Laboratories cyber security poster.

FIGURE 7.2

Potential targeted malware infection lures.

As with any of the other aspects of intelligence-led security discussed in this book, security awareness training is most effective when it is fully supported to by leadership within the organization. If users perceive leadership is fully committed, they are more likely to take it seriously. Therefore, security awareness training should be included as part of any security plan, it should be seen as an integral part of the security program, which it is.

One thing to consider when developing a security awareness training program is the inclusion of trusted security vendors in that program. Oftentimes, having another party come in to discuss trends in cyber threats and how those trends impact the organization adds impact to the conversation. That being said, outside vendors will never replace the security team as the experts on security within the organization. But a speaker from a security vendor can offer a different perspective. Many security vendors are happy to offer this service at no cost to their customers.

CUSTOMER SECURITY AWARENESS TRAINING

Depending on the nature of the organization, it may make sense to provide security awareness to training to customers as well as employees. Many organizations do this today and it not only improves the entire security ecosystem it can also generate valuable intelligence.

Consumer-facing organizations have known this for a while. Financial institutions regularly send email to their customers letting them know about the latest phishing scams, retail companies send out emails reminding customers that they will never the customer to send a password via email, and email providers send out warnings about potential threats to their customers' accounts and data.

In addition to warning customers, the organization should ask their customers to forward them suspicious email. Whereas employee reporting should done through systems that can integrate directly into security collecting platform, simply asking customers to forward suspicious emails should be enough. On the backend, there should be a way to integrate those emails into the security analytics platform in a programmatic way. But, all of that should be invisible to the customer.

Repeating the "if you see something, say something" mantra to your customers will, as with the employees of the organization, keep security always in the back of their mind. Having customers forward samples of suspicious or phishing emails that appear to be related to the organization greatly improves the attack surface that the security team is able to monitor. It also lets customers know that the organization takes security very seriously and it provides additional campaign information that can be compiled and shared internally as well as delivered back to the customers.

OpenIOC, CyBOX, STIX, and TAXII

In the realm of vulnerability intelligence most organizations rely heavily on the Security Content Automation Protocol (SCAP) to share vulnerability information between platforms. SCAP is an efficient way of sharing vulnerability information, but it does not really work for sharing cyber threat data. Organizations that rely on multiple sources of intelligence and want to join those sources into a single platform need a common language and structure.

The good news is that there are number of emerging standards that allow organizations to normalize threat intelligence data across all platforms within the organization. Threat intelligence languages and frameworks are also being used by intelligence providers to programmatically deliver security data directly into client systems. Two examples of this type integration discussed in Chapter 6 are YARA (see p. 0000) and CRITs (see p. 0000).

OpenIOC

One of the first tools is OpenIOC (www.openioc.org), which is a framework originally developed my Mandiant (www.mandiant.com), but released as an open platform that everyone can use. OpenIOC is a framework for cataloging indicators of compromise associated with malware. The OPenIOC framework uses an XML-based schema, similar to this snippet[1]:

[1]Snippet taken from the OpenIOC Schema at http://schemas.mandiant.com/2010/ioc/ioc.xsd (accessed 18.09.14.).

```
<xs:element name="ioc" nillable="true"
type="tns:IndicatorOfCompromise"/>
<xs:complexType name="IndicatorOfCompromise">
<xs:sequence>
<xs:element minOccurs="0" maxOccurs="1"
name="short_description" type="xs:string"/>
<xs:element minOccurs="0" maxOccurs="1" name="description"
type="xs:string"/>
<xs:element minOccurs="0" maxOccurs="1" name="keywords"
type="xs:string"/>
<xs:element minOccurs="0" maxOccurs="1" name="authored_by"
type="xs:string"/>
<xs:element minOccurs="1" maxOccurs="1"
name="authored_date" nillable="true" type="xs:dateTime"/>
<xs:element minOccurs="0" maxOccurs="1" name="links"
type="tns:ArrayOfLink"/>
<xs:element minOccurs="0" maxOccurs="1" name="definition"
type="tns:ArrayOfIocIndicator"/>
</xs:sequence>
<xs:attribute name="id" type="xs:string"/>
<xs:attribute name="last-modified" type="xs:dateTime"
use="required"/>
</xs:complexType>
```

OpenIOC allows an organization to track indicators of compromise (IOC) across multiple platforms and tie behaviors associated with those IOCs together with the IOC. This enables security analysts to tie operational and tactical data together in a single framework.

CyBOX

Cyber Observable eXpression (cybox.mitre.org) is a framework developed by Mitre (www.mitre.org) to manage communication and reporting of cyber observables, another way of saying indicators. Out of the box, CyBOX takes a much broader view of what constitutes an indicator than OpenIOC (though OpenIOC is designed to be extensible). CyBOX looks for what it terms measurable or stateful events. A measurable event is a new registry key added, the hash of a file changing, or a file being deleted. Stateful events are those that are constant, such as a file hash, the registry entry itself or a domain name.

CyBOX creates different objects for each type of observable, allowing for variance depending on the nature of the indicator. While this makes it a more complex framework than OpenIOC it does allow for context around the observable to be shared.[2]

---

[2]Taken from the CyBOX Patterns Example page at http://cybox.mitre.org/about/example_patterns.html (accessed 18.09.14.).

```
<cybox:Observables
xmlns:xsi="http://www.w3.org/2001/XMLSchema-instance"
    xmlns:cybox="http://cybox.mitre.org/cybox-2"
    xmlns:cyboxCommon="http://cybox.mitre.org/common-2"


xmlns:URIObject="http://cybox.mitre.org/objects#URIOb
ject-2"
    xmlns:example="http://example.com/"
    xsi:schemaLocation="
    http://cybox.mitre.org/cybox-2 ../cybox_core.xsd
    http://cybox.mitre.org/objects#URIObject-2
../objects/URI_Object.xsd"
    cybox_major_version="2" cybox_minor_version="0">
    <cybox:Observable id="example:Observable-1c9af310-
0d5a-4c44-bdd7-aea3d99f13b6">
        <cybox:Object id="example:Object-26be6630-b2df-
4bf9-8750-3f45ca9e19cf">
            <cybox:Properties
xsi:type="URIObject:URIObjectType">
                <URIObject:Value condition="Equals"
apply_condition="Any">
www.sample1.com/index.html,sample2.com/login.html,dev
.sample3.com/index/kb.html </URIObject:Value>
            </cybox:Properties>
        </cybox:Object>
    </cybox:Observable>
</cybox:Observables>
```

STIX AND TAXII

Structured Threat Information eXpression (STIX) and Trusted Automated eXchange of Indicator Information (TAXII) are, respectively, a language for conveying cyber threat intelligence information and transport mechanism over which to share cyber threat information. While STIX (stix.mitre.org) and TAXII (taxii.mitre.org) are usually mentioned in the same breath, they are actually two very different things.

STIX is a language for communicating the operational, tactical, and strategic information about a threat in a standardized way that can be ingested using a variety of security tools. In other words, it provides actor, tactics, and infrastructure information to in a single package that can be shared across an organization or with other organizations.

The language can be structured in a number of ways, as long as it includes the proper elements, a snipped of a typical STIX report looks like this[3]:

```
<stix:STIX_Header>
      <stix:Title>Example watchlist that contains domain
information.</stix:Title>
      <stix:Package_Intent
xsi:type="stixVocabs:PackageIntentVocab-1.0">Indicators -
Watchlist</stix:Package_Intent>
      </stix:STIX_Header>
      <stix:Indicators>
      <stix:Indicator xsi:type="indicator:IndicatorType"
id="example:Indicator-2e20c5b2-56fa-46cd-9662-8f199c69d2c9"
timestamp="2014-05-08T09:00:00.000000Z">
            <indicator:Type
xsi:type="stixVocabs:IndicatorTypeVocab-1.1">Domain
Watchlist</indicator:Type>
            <indicator:Description>Sample domain Indicator
for this watchlist</indicator:Description>
            <indicator:Observable id="example:Observable-
87c9a5bb-d005-4b3e-8081-99f720fad62b">
                  <cybox:Object id="example:Object-12c760ba-
cd2c-4f5d-a37d-18212eac7928">
                        <cybox:Properties
xsi:type="DomainNameObj:DomainNameObjectType" type="FQDN">

                        <DomainNameObj:Value
condition="Equals"
apply_condition="ANY">malicious1.example.com##comma##mali
cious2.example.com##comma##malicious3.example.com</Domain
NameObj:Value>
                  </cybox:Properties>
            </cybox:Object>
      </indicator:Observable>
      </stix:Indicator>
      </stix:Indicators>
```

[3]Taken from the STIX Report sample page at http://stix.mitre.org/language/version1.0.1/samples/ STIX_Domain_Watchlist.html (accessed 18.09.14.).

By default, STIX uses the CyBOX schema to describe observables within the language. In fact the CyBOX schema is imported natively.

That being said, STIX is extensible, and for organizations that prefer to use OpenIOC, STIX does provide a default extension for OpenIOC. STIX also provides an extension for YARA rules.

TAXII, on the other hand, is a transport mechanism. It provides protocols for sharing cyber threat intelligence, but it can be used for other types of data sharing as well. TAXII has four core services: Discovery, Feed Management, Poll, and Inbox. The Discovery service is about determining the method of communication between other TAXII hosts. The Feed Management service is about managing data subscriptions. Poll and Inbox are about the pushing and pulling of data to the source, respectively.

TAXII is not a transfer protocol; instead it binds itself to HTTP and HTTPS, allowing those protocols to conduct the transfer. Version 1.0 of TAXII also limits its message bindings to XML.

In essence, TAXII is a mechanism for delivering intelligence messaging, using XML, over an HTTP/HTTPS connection. That being said, TAXII is not limited to any of those aspects of communication, it is simply its primary purpose at this time.

THREAT INTELLIGENCE MANAGEMENT PLATFORMS

Having emerging standards and getting threat intelligence partners to support those standards, the next step is finding a central repository where that data can be stored as it proceeds through the intelligence cycle.

In this case, a SIEM is not usually enough. Many cyber threat intelligence providers have done an admirable job of trying to shoehorn threat intelligence into SIEM platforms, but it is not usually a good fit for reasons discussed earlier.

In essence, intelligence-led security organizations often outgrow their SIEMs, which creates a problem because so much invaluable data is contained within those SIEMs and most organizations build their security programs around their SIEMs.

That is where a relatively new category of security systems comes into play. Gartner refers to these platforms as threat intelligence management platforms (TIMPs). TIMPs are built from the ground up to support the correlation of threat intelligence, which includes being able to ingest data in STIX, OpenIOC, and other threat intelligence languages and frameworks.

Adopting a TIMP within the network does not mean abandoning a SIEM in which an organization has invested heavily. In fact, TIMPs are not designed to replace a SIEM; instead, they are built to work with the data contained within the SIEM. A security analyst can build a finished report merging indicators from multiple sources and deliver that information directly into the SIEM, as in Figure 7.3.

This customized view of a suspected campaign gives the security analyst even more control over the types of indicators delivered into the SIEM for correlation. It also means that, using internally collected data, the security analyst can flesh out the

FIGURE 7.3

Viewing multiple campaigns in the ThreatQuotient (ThreatQ) console.

reports from multiple threat-intelligence providers and build a FINTEL product that is unique to that organization.

There are a number of young companies that are jumping into this new category. Just some of the vendors are ThreatQuotient (www.threatquotient.com), Threat-Stream (www.threatstream.com), Centripetal Networks (www.centripetalnetworks.com), ThreatConnect (www.threatconnect.com),[4] and VorStack (www.vorstack.com). There are also established security vendors who are moving into this space, like BAE Systems (www.bae.com) with the Detica CyberReveal®. There is also a project under the FS-ISAC called Soltra (www.soltra.com), that is a combination of TIMP and information sharing platform.

TIMPs solve a number of problems that have plagued early adopters of cyber threat intelligence and organizations moving toward IGCND. The most important one is the SIEM problem outlined above, but SIEMs are not the only recipients of cyber threat intelligence within the network.

Previous chapters have discussed intelligence integration into network monitoring platforms, web proxies, firewalls, Domain Name System (DNS) servers, incident response tools, intrusion detection systems, and more. There are a few different ways

---

[4]Notice a naming pattern here?

this can be done, but the most common way it is done today is to integrate each intelligence data feed into multiple platforms. The same intelligence data, from multiple providers, is ingested across multiple platforms within the organization.

This model creates a lot of duplication within the organization and it takes control of intelligence distribution within the organization away from the security team leaves it in the hands of the cyber threat intelligence providers. By using a TIMP to centralize the collection of external cyber threat intelligence data the security team regains control. A security analyst can sort through the relevant indicators from a variety of sources and use that information to build a YARA signature. She can then push that YARA signature to the platforms to which it applies.

Some intelligence data needs to be delivered to some platforms, but not others. Using the TIMP as the central repository, the security team now has the ability to build alerts using standardized language and can control where it is delivered. Again, this gives the security team the ability to inject itself into the kill chain as early possible, so it is not using intelligence within the SIEM to tag events postcompromise.

Using a TIMP platform can increase the efficiency of the security organization in an intelligence-led security program. Today, security analysts spend a great deal of time manually coordinating threats from multiple intelligence vendors. There is a lot of cutting and pasting and note taking that interferes with the work of actually securing the organization. This work is a necessary, but tedious, aspect of an intelligence-led security organization.

By normalizing the cyber threat intelligence from multiple vendors a TIMP speeds up the processes of correlating information and reduces the amount of cutting and pasting and note taking that needs to be done manually. Within the TIMP the security team has the ability to coordinate data from multiple sources, add notes directly into the platform and quickly produce the desired output. Again, they can even stream that information, notes and all, into the targeted platform. The notes are particularly useful, so when the intelligence does result in an alert the on-duty analyst will have immediate context as well as a reference point as to where to go look for more information.

TIMPs AS A ROSETTA STONE

Sun Tzu said, "Thus, what enables the wise sovereign and the good general to strike and conquer, and achieve things beyond the reach of ordinary men, is foreknowledge." In this passage, Sun Tzu is talking specifically about spies, but the broader point is getting to know the enemy and understand how the enemy operates.

This need to understand the actors behind the threat is what is very quickly driving intelligence-led security to be adversary focused. Focusing on the adversary allows organizations to tie all of the different indicators together to produce focused operational intelligence, but it also allows security teams to connect that operational intelligence to the tactical intelligence by tying those indicators to tools and infrastructure used in attacks. Finally, both the indicators and the tools can be tied to a group. That group may not be known at first, but by continuing to track the activity more and more information about that group becomes apparent and attribution can be guessed.

This is what cyber threat intelligence providers do, some with greater success than others. They combine open source intelligence (OSINT), signals intelligence (SIGINT), and, in some cases, human-sourced intelligence (HUMINT) to paint pictures of these different groups and their associated tactics and indicators. Once all of this information has been collected it is published to their clients in report format as either a PDF, an email delivery, or delivered through the Application Programming Interface (API).

That is when the problem starts for the clients. An organization may have three or four different threat-intelligence providers sharing the same information under different adversary names. Figure 7.3 demonstrates this problem well. A security analyst has uncovered the domain weather-online.hopto.org within the organization. The analyst thinks it is suspicious so the analyst enters it into the analyst's ThreatQuotient management platforms and the analyst's suspicions are confirmed. The analyst sees that the domain has been confirmed as malicious, but one organization refers to the actor as SNAKE, while the second refers to it as ENERGETIC BEAR.

This may be the most powerful use case for a TIMP within the organization. Not only can the TIMP tie together indicators from across multiple threat intelligence solutions, it can also be used to tie campaign information from across multiple cyber threat intelligence providers. Remember that no one threat-intelligence provider is able to monitor everything that is happening on, and off, the Internet. Quite often, one intelligence provider will see one aspect of an attack, while another will see a different aspect. Combining the two sources of information can provide an organization with a more complete view of the attack.

Unfortunately, intelligence providers make combining datasets challenging by assigning different names to the adversaries they are tracking. Considering that the adversaries are assigned different names and providers have different views of the activity of those adversaries, it is challenging for their customers to determine which group from one provider matches a group from another provider. Again, it requires a lot of manual effort on the part of the client to match indicators, tactics, and any other aspects known about the groups.

That is where the Rosetta Stone–like capabilities of TIMPs have the potential to excel. The TIMP is already synthesizing data from multiple sources and normalizing it for distribution throughout the network. The TIMP can also be used to isolate groupings of indicators and match them from one provider to another (shown in Figure 7.3) thus presenting a cross section of indicators from different providers all tied to the same actor in an automated fashion.

A caveat to this is that the process will never be perfect. One cyber threat intelligence provider may assign an indicator to one group while another provider assigns it to a completely different group. Not just different group names, but groups with completely different attributes. For example, one provider may tie an indicator to an actor operating out of Estonia, while another may tie that same indicator to a group operating out of India. Of course, that doesn't mean that one or both threat-intelligence providers are wrong. With the explosion of malicious activity around the world and a limited number of vulnerable hosts (it is still a very large number), it is not uncommon for the same host to be compromised by two different actors and used for redirection by both of those malicious actors.

If the first provider noted traffic originating from the compromised host that mirrored activity seen from the Estonian group while the second provider could be seeing activity from the same host that matches tactics, techniques, and procedures (TTPs) from the group in India. Even though it is rare that there will be a one-to-one match of indicator sets associated with actors from one cyber threat intelligence provider to another, the TIMP can still simplify the process of connecting groups across providers.

This actually ties to one of the biggest complaints that cyber threat intelligence consumers have: why can't cyber threat intelligence providers create a Rosetta Stone on their own? This is similar to the problem that antivirus vendors face 20+ years ago. Symantec would label a virus as one thing, while McAfee would refer to it by a different name, Kaspersky would have yet a third name and so on. Security teams that were struggling to keep up with latest virus outbreaks were very frustrated (sound familiar?) trying to track threats across the organization and around the world. Antivirus vendors got together and agreed to sharing naming information, making it easier to find the name of a piece of malicious code across all providers. That has worked very well for these providers for several decades now.

Unfortunately, it is not as easy to do this with cyber threat intelligence. There is a lot of intellectual property involved in building an intelligence collection infrastructure and creating reporting that is delivered to clients. Sharing malicious actor information involves more than just sharing a file hash. In order to truly share information cyber threat intelligence providers would have to disclose all of the attributes discussed throughout this book. At this point there isn't an effective way to manage sharing and protect the intellectual property of the cyber threat intelligence providers.

BIG DATA SECURITY ANALYTICS

The term *big data* is everywhere. It seems every security company today is talking about a big data solution or something they are doing to further enhance big data solutions. Through all of the marketing hype, there are excellent reasons for some organizations to look at a big data solution for their environment.

Big data security analytics is really an answer to the question asked in Chapter 5: how much data should an organization collect for security analysis? In the big data security analytics model, the answer to that question is: everything.

In the traditional GRC and SIEM collection model, log data has to be massaged for it to be delivered into the platform – the platform needs to know what it is ingesting to be able to act upon it. These solutions are also often limited in terms of the amount of data they can successfully ingest and process in a timely fashion. Any security analyst that has ever worked with a SIEM that is nearing database capacity knows this feeling: Enter in a search query, head out for a nice long lunch, come back, stop to chat with coworkers, get back to the desk and see the search results are still not presented. In an intelligence-led security organization those types of waits are unacceptable.

Big data analytics solutions like HP's Vertica (www.vertica.com), IBM's Netezza (www.ibm.com), Palantir (www.palantir.com), and Splunk (www.splunk.com) operate in a different manner.

To start with, the underlying databases used in these solutions have already been implemented across a wide range of high-volume, high-transaction sectors, such as finance and retail. Because of this background, they are well suited for high volumes of data collection from a range of sources, which means that they can handle large amounts of data, process that data quickly, and return search results in a timely fashion.

Big data solutions are also used to dealing with nebulous data types. Most SIEMs will choke on data that does not conform to a specific type or exists outside of a specific framework. While having a structured framework across all platforms makes for easier correlation, it also runs the risk that not all data will be included.

When a security vendor restricts their data to a limited framework that sometimes means having to drop fields in order to support that framework. So, while the vendor may log a great deal of contextual information a lot of it might be lost when it is converted to syslog or CEF formats. The plus side is that the conversion makes it easier to correlate logs and other data across multiple platforms if they are all in the same format.

With big data security analytics, that is no longer a concern. The big data solution ingests the data natively and builds objects around the data, it also allows for unstructured data to be ingested into the solution. This means instead of a dataset limited by the capabilities of the SIEM or GRC, pointers to all of the data resides within the database. Now security analysts can write queries based on what they want to know.

But wait – being a security analyst does make someone a database expert. A security analyst may have gone her entire career without writing anything more than a few MySQL queries; all of a sudden the analyst is expected to write a bunch of queries to this database?

Absolutely not, that is really where the security analytics part of the big data security analytics solutions comes in to play. Vendors that are offering big data security analytics solutions put a front-end to the database that manages many of the typical relational queries that can provide security value. On top of that, most of the vendors offer outsourced expertise with these queries and can help create custom rule sets based on the specific security systems within the network as well as the security goals of the organization. Of course, this expertise usually comes with a cost.

The real value in a big data security analytics system that is properly deployed and contains the right datasets is the ability to detect anomalous events. Ultimately, that is the goal when trying to detect events outside of those that match signatures or indicators: highlight activities in the organization that simply don't "feel right."

Some types of anomalous traffic detection were discussed in Chapter 6 (see p. 0000), but a big data security analytics solution can take the discovery of these anomalous events to the next level. Yes, these solutions do require a great deal more caring and feeding than a traditional SIEM or GRC solution, but the possibilities for incident detection are vastly improved.

HADOOP

Hadoop (hadoop.apache.org) is an open source scalable solution for distributed computing that allows organizations to spread computing power across a large number of systems. The goal with Hadoop is to be able to process large amounts of data simultaneously and return results quickly. Hadoop is a very powerful tool, with a wide range of resources, including security analytics.

The Hadoop framework solves some of the problems with SIEM and GRC platforms mentioned earlier. Because of its distributed nature, Hadoop is able to process a lot of log and unstructured data in a very timely fashion and return those results. That being said, Hadoop is not a database, instead it is a storage and processing system. What that means is that can take data transactions in whatever form and allow the organization to process those transactions across commodity hardware.

Several security vendors, such as RSA (www.rsa.com) and Splunk (www.splunk.com) have already seen the value that Hadoop can bring to security and provide front security front ends to the Hadoop framework.

CONCLUSION

Correlating data collected internally with a variety of external sources of information and fusing that into a single stream of FINTEL presents a significant challenge to any organization. However, mastering gaining control over these varied datasets significantly improves security across the organization, by increasing situational awareness and response to security events.

One way to improve that fusion is by using emerging cyber threat standards such as OpenIOC, CyBOX, STIX, and TAXII to ensure that all sources of security sharing are communicating using the same framework.

Another option is to use a TIMP as a clearinghouse for all threat intelligence data. The TIMP platform can then translate the different forms of data inputs into a single fused output that can be programmatically delivered to the appropriate security systems.

An alternative, and at times significantly more complex, solution is to migrate to a big data security analytics platform. Big data security analytics platforms are great for collecting any and all data in its raw format in order to provide full context of a security event. Correlation is done based on an understanding of the data structures, rather than forcing the data to comply to the platform structure. These platforms provide a security-focused front end that manages much of the querying and analysis through an easy to use front end. Thus ensuring that security analysts don't need to be database experts as well.

Whatever methods an organization uses to tie all data sources together into a singular format that can be distributed throughout the network, there will absolutely be improvements in the security posture of the organization.

REFERENCE

Tzu, S. The Art of War, (Lionel Giles, Trans.). Polity, New York, p. 50.

CERTs, ISACs, and intelligence-sharing communities

INTRODUCTION

Building out an intelligence-led security program is hard; doing it alone is almost impossible. The good news is that most organizations do not have to do it alone. Other organizations in the same space are either going through the same challenges, or have gone through those challenges. By collaborating with other organizations in the same vertical everyone within that vertical can improve their security posture and develop better situational awareness around the threats.

Collaborating with other organizations regarding cyber security issues is scary proposition to many organizations. Even if the security team is willing to share information many leaders in the organization will be afraid of the legal ramifications and the obligation to the organization's stakeholders. There is still a stigma associated with cyber security breaches that many organizational leaders fear.

The fact is that just about every organization in every vertical has been breached. It might be something as simple as commodity malware that Bob in Human Resources infected his machine with while playing a Flash-based Pac-Man, or it might be a targeted attack, but every network has malware on it. Sharing data with other organizations inside and outside of the organization's vertical helps everyone else. One organization's breach is another's predictive intelligence.

Despite what some security vendors like to claim, no one organization understands every cyber threat. No one organization has complete visibility to the Internet and all of the Tor-enabled forums. Which means, that no matter how well an organization prepares for attacks, there are going to be things that get through. Understanding the attacks that eluded a competitor's defenses helps improve everyone else's chances of protecting against that threat.

There are different ways to share data, different types of data to share and different security organizations that specialize in the sharing and dissemination of security intelligence. The three that are the focus of this chapter are Computer Emergency

Response Teams (CERTs)/Computer Security Incident Response Teams (CSIRTs), Information Sharing and Analysis Centers (ISACs), and cyber intelligence communities.

These organization range from CERTs, which are authoritative with very little collaborations, to ISACs, which are industry-sponsored and more collaborative, to cyber intelligence communities, which are completely collaborative and sometimes ad-hoc.

Working with these different entities improves exposure to the different threats affecting businesses and the government and it can provide special insight into those threats targeting specific industries. But to take advantage of the wealth of data, oftentimes a change in culture is needed within the organization. Making that change is worth it for the additional intelligence gained.

CERTs AND CSIRTs

The primary purpose of CERTs and CSIRTs is to coordinate and disseminate cyber security information within an entity. That entity could be a company, agency, a group of companies/agencies, a state, country or the world. CERTs are generally looking for broad security events that impact large swathes of their users. Sometimes the users are security teams in an organization and sometimes the users are the end users. CERTs generally serve as a clearinghouse and usually function almost like a funnel. They take in a great deal of information, coordinate that information, and release the results in a manageable format that is easily digestible by the widest possible audience.

CERTs do not serve as incident response team (usually); instead, they work with incident results teams to coordinate their findings with other security vendors and other incident response teams to deliver an alert. The CERT is supposed to see the big picture: similar attacks are happening at organizations A, B, and Q. The CERT can help determine if it is a coincidence or part of an ongoing campaign. Used correctly and with a willingness to share, a CERT can be a powerful tool that improves the security for everyone.

CERT/COORDINATION CENTER

The first CSIRT was the Carnegie CERT/Coordination Center (CERT/CC). The CERT/CC (http://www.cert.org) is part of the Software Engineering Institute (SEI) affiliated with Carnegie Mellon University. Interestingly, in the case of the CERT/CC, CERT is not an acronym; it is simply the name of the organization.

The CERT/CC was founded in 1988 to coordinate the efforts to combat the Morris worm that had taken down much of the fledgling Internet (see Chapter 1, p. 0000, for more details). The mission for the CERT/CC has been remained the same since its founding: To serve as a coordination center during cyber threat emergencies and wide-scale security events.

One of the services that CERT/CC provides is current vulnerability information within their Vulnerability Notes Database (available at http://www.kb.cert.org/vuls/), including information on how networks can protect themselves from the disclosed vulnerabilities. CERT/CC conducts original research on vulnerabilities, in addition to its coordination with entities that may have discovered vulnerabilities in their network and the vendors who might be impacted.

But the role of CERT/CC goes well beyond vulnerability research. It also provides security teams with information to improve the security of their networks, improve situational awareness, conduct forensic analysis, protect against malicious insider threats, perform better risk management, and code in-house applications more securely. For each of the subject areas that CERT/CC covers, it provides tools, research papers, and best practices information that can be invaluable to security teams.

CERT/CC offers services that go beyond simple coordination as well. It offers a range of risk assessment services that offer security teams that are struggling a chance to understand areas that need improvement and what needs to be done to move toward an intelligence-led security program. It also offers a number of training classes that will improve the security posture of new members of a team, or serve as a refresher for senior members. However an organization decides to use the myriad of resources available from CERT/CC, it should absolutely be a part of any security arsenal.

US-CERT AND COUNTRY-LEVEL CSIRTs

The United States Computer Emergency Readiness Team (US-CERT) is responsible for coordinating the cyber security information that impacts every government agency, business, and individual computer user in the United States. Like the CERT/CC, US-CERT (https://www.us-cert.gov/) provides security alerts, vulnerability information and helpful tips for protecting an organization or a home user. It also has a series of mailing lists that anyone can join to find out information about the latest threats on which the US-CERT is reporting. These mailing lists are one-way, the US-CERT uses them to disseminate information, and they are not meant for discussion purposes.

The US-CERT also allows constituents to report information via phone, email, or by using a secure incident reporting Web form on its Web site. The US-CERT accepts reports of security incidents, phishing attempts, malware and vulnerability reporting, and potential vulnerabilities on United States Government Web sites.

The US-CERT also coordinates information with the defense and intelligence communities within the United States. It also has information sharing agreements with other countries, which allows it to quickly assess the impact of a security event around the world.

The United States is not the only country with a national CERT. There are a number of them that are very active and have a unique perspective on threats within their company. France has CERT-FR (http://cert.ssi.gouv.fr). In Australia there is the AusCERT (http://www.auscert.org.au), the Australian Computer Emergency

Response Team. In the United Kingdom the CSIRT is CERT UK (https://www.cert.gov.uk). Japan has the JPCERT/CC, the Japan Computer Emergency Response Team Coordination Center (https://www.jpcert.or.jp).

Awareness of the CSIRT organizations within other countries is important, especially for organizations that have offices or employees stationed or traveling to those countries. While some threats are universal, there are others that seem to be targeting specific countries, or even specific industries within those countries. A lot of the differences are based on the adversary and where the adversary is targeting the adversary's attacks. There is also a difference in attacks based on technology adoption. For example, although Huawei phones are very popular in some parts of the world, they are hardly used at all in other parts. A vulnerability targeting Huawei phones may be a serious problem in India, but not as serious a problem in France. Again, tracking the threats in other countries helps security teams maintain good situational awareness and disseminate the relevant intelligence to employees who have a need to know.

Tracking down country-level CSIRTs can be done through FIRST (http://www.first.org). FIRST is a forum for CSIRTs at both the country and company level. It is an organization with more than 250 members and a place where CSIRTs around the world can share information and learn about best practices from other CSIRTs. While it is true that CERT/CC has been around since 1988, most CSIRTs have not been around that long. Surprisingly, some large countries have had a national CSIRT for fewer than 5 years. Having the FIRST forum available helps get new countries and companies up to speed when setting up their CSIRTs, and quickly gets them engaged in working with the rest of the CSIRT community.

COMPANY-LEVEL CSIRTs

Many technology companies also have their own CSIRTs that supply their clients with information about the latest threats against their platforms and serve as a coordination center for those who want to report new vulnerabilities. Aggregate vulnerability feeds were discussed in chapter 6, but company CSIRTs can often offer additional insights into threats and they provide a chance for their customers to interact directly with experts from the vendor.

One of the best examples of this is the Cisco Product Security Incident Response Team (Cisco PSIRT). The Cisco PSIRT has been running continuously since 1995 and provides easy access to their customers, or anyone with an interest, to the latest threats affecting Cisco devices. Their web portal (http://www.cisco.com/go/psirt/) is easy to search and includes easy-to-find contact information for organizations that are under attack or having other security issues where they need a Cisco expert.

Intel is another technology company that takes security very seriously. Intel has set up the Intel FIRST team (https://security-center.intel.com) to inform customers of vulnerabilities in and potential threats against Intel technologies. Like Cisco, the Intel FIRST portal provides information about how to contact the Intel FIRST team to report new vulnerabilities or if there is a security problems with Intel products.

It is not just companies that make technology products that have CSIRTS, most Internet Service Providers (ISPs) also have active CSIRTs to handle customer problems, as well as reports from thirds parties about malicious traffic leaving the ISP's network. Verizon, Comcast, AT&T, and other ISPs all have active CSIRTs that will work with clients as well as victims of attacks that appear to be originating from their networks.

Beyond technology companies and ISPs, many other companies with a large Internet presence also maintain active CSIRTs to respond to threats targeting their users. Companies like Google, Facebook, PayPal, and Yahoo all have strong CSIRTs that are able to adapt quickly to reported threats as well as actively monitor for, and quickly remove, threats to their users. These threats can ranges from malicious users on their networks, to phishing attacks against their users, to malware embedded into applications, to flaws within the platform itself. Even at the corporate level, companies like SalesForce.com and SAP maintain active CSIRTs that are on constant alert for threats against companies using their services.

Given the large number of phishing attacks targeting banking customers it should come as no surprise that banking organizations maintain some of the most robust and responsive CSIRT organizations. Bank of America, Deutsche Bank, BNP Paribas, National Australia Bank, and Visa, among many others, have strong CSIRTs that handle queries about suspected phishing attacks, actively monitor underground forums for the sale of their banking customer credentials, watch for new attacks, and understand what type of future attacks might impact their clients. Given the importance of financial data to their customers financial institution CSIRTs in particular rely on intelligence to provide proactive security which enables them to get ahead of new threats.

ISACs

CERTs are a great source of security information that affects a large group of people and organizations. Some of the CERTs even provide what can be considered finished intelligence (FINTEL).[1] But information from CERTs is rarely, by design, focused on a specific organization or sector. That is where the ISACs take over.

ISACs are industry-focused communities that allow members to share cyber security information. But, ISACs don't just focus on cyber security threats; they also monitor physical and any other potential threats to the industry.

The concept of an ISAC was developed during the Clinton Administration and released as Presidential Decision Directive-63 (PDD-63), the full capabilities of the ISACs were later refined under President Bush with Homeland Security Presidential Directive 7 (HSPD-7, 2003). ISACs were formed specifically to increase situational awareness of the threats surrounding the critical infrastructure sectors. Even in 1998

---

[1]For example, the ICS-CERT releases what they call Joint Security Awareness Reports (https://ics-cert.us-cert.gov/jsars/) that go into detail about specific threats to Industrial Control Systems.

the ISACs were aware of the threat against cyber infrastructure and this was called out in PDD-63 (1998):

> *"Many of the nation's critical infrastructures have historically been physically and logically separate systems that had little interdependence. As a result of advances in information technology and the necessity of improved efficiency, however, these infrastructures have become increasingly automated and interlinked. These same advances have created new vulnerabilities to equipment failure, human error, weather and other natural causes, and physical and cyber attacks."*

The ISACs serve several roles on behalf of their constituents and their liaisons within the federal government. Their primary purpose is to serve as a clearinghouse for its members, providing sector-specific alerts, intelligence requirements, and intelligence dissemination regarding threats and vulnerabilities. Each ISAC also works closely with its liaisons within the government to help the attached agencies better understand the threats facing that particular vertical. The ISAC also serves as a secure communication platform where members can share indicators and get feedback from other members. Finally, the ISAC also provides emergency response capability to Federal Agencies during widespread attacks that are specifically impacting the industry.

Each ISAC maintains a CSIRT that operates 24×7 to support needs of the members and to help them quickly respond to new threats as well as inform other members about the threat. Industry experts staff the CSIRTs for the individual ISACs, so they not only understand the cyber security landscape, but they also understand the specific vertical threats. This type of staffing gives ISAC members access to unique, focused, data as well as finished intelligence that applies to their specific networks.

It also provides a chance to gain better contextual information around a threat. A file hash that looks like commodity malware to a Web Application Firewall, but is also being used against five other organizations in the same vertical suddenly becomes more interesting. By opening lines of communication between members the ISACs improving security for all members and creating better situational awareness.

Running a 24×7 CSIRT on behalf of their members also means that if the Department of Homeland Security (DHS) through the US-CERT, or any of the intelligence or law enforcement agencies need to communicate a potential threat to a particular sector there is a single point of contact to which that agency needs to reach out. For example the Financial Services (FS)-ISAC, with more than 5000 members, has immediate access to more than 99% of the banks and credit unions within the United States. A single call to the FS-ISAC CSIRT means that the cyber threat information is relayed quickly and more than 90% of the financial sector will have the information needed to protect their networks.

Since PDD-63 was released in 1998, there have a number of ISACs created to meet specific sector needs. As these ISACs have grown and continue to grow they have become invaluable assets to their members, proving a great deal of raw data and FINTEL to their members. But, ISACs serve a broader purpose as well. They are also responsible for ensuring that their members are able to communicate with each other.

To that end, many of the ISACs have been big proponents of standards that facilitate the communication of cyber threat information between their members as well as other organizations. In particular the FS-ISAC has been instrumental in pushing the STIX, TAXII, and CyBOX standards originally developed by MITRE.

Of course, different ISACs are at different levels of development. Those that have been around for 10 or more years are, for the most part, very sophisticated and deliver invaluable data and intelligence to their members. The newer ISACs are still building out capability, but with the strong blueprint provided by the more established ISACs, they are able to quickly get up to speed.

In fact, the ISACs created an organization called the National Council of ISACs (http://www.isaccouncil.org/) in 2003 to help ISAC members address common problems facing each ISAC. The National Council of ISACs (NCI) serves as a clearinghouse of information for all of the ISACs. The NCI is made up of four representatives from each of the member ISACs plus a leadership team. They offer an information-sharing portal for the ISACs to share information, and they work with industries interested in setting up an ISAC.

Information sharing between ISACs is critical because it is rare that a threat or adversary focuses on a single sector. An adversary generally has a limited toolset or, at least, favors a group of tools. That adversary is usually attacking multiple sectors in multiple countries. By comparing data between ISACs, members can learn about the adversary's tactical and operational techniques before she launches attacks against their sector. An actor using a new variant of ZeuS on Monday to target companies in the financial industry may be using the same ZeuS variant (not to mention the same infrastructure) in 3 weeks to attacks companies in the defense industrial base (DIB). By comparing notes, members of the DIB will be aware of what to expect and its members will be able to take proper precautions.

The NCI also serves as a liaison with the National Cybersecurity & Communications Integration Center (NCCIC). The NCCIC is the center within DHS that is responsible for securing the national infrastructure. It operates a 24×7 CSIRT that maintains situational awareness and incident response and serves as a clearinghouse of cyber security incidents for the rest of DHS, law enforcement and the intelligence community.

THE ISACs

As mentioned, there are a number of ISACs spanning across a range of industries. This section covers some of the better known ISACs.

The FS-ISAC (https://www.fsisac.com) is one of the largest and best known ISACs. With more than 5000 members, the CSIRT within the FS-ISAC processes thousands of events each month on behalf of its members. Sifting through those thousands of events, the FS-ISAC is able to submit 40 incidents to its members, ISAC partners, and to its government liaisons each month.

Because the FS-ISAC was one of the first ISACs formed under PDD-63, its members were forced to design processes and build systems that would satisfy the PDD and improve the security of their members. Fortunately, with a strong leadership team and a sense of urgency from their member financial services organizations the FS-ISAC has been able to quickly mature into one of the most effective ISACs in terms of cyber security and producing relevant cyber threat intelligence for its members. As new industry ISACs are formed many choose to copy some or all of what the FS-ISAC has accomplished.

Another example of a successful, though not as well known, ISAC is the Information Technology (IT)-ISAC (http://www.it-isac.org/). The IT-ISAC was founded in 2000 to support companies in the information technology sector. The IT-ISAC serves members such as Hewlett-Packard, Intel, Oracle, Symantec, Cisco, FireEye, Workday, and many more technology and security companies. By serving as neutral third party for an industry that can be fiercely competitive, the IT-ISAC helps members understand how threats can impact not just their networks but also the products they are selling to people or organizations. A security flaw in a product of one member of the IT-ISAC can impact millions, or even billions, of people if it is not quickly addressed and a patch issued in a timely fashion.

For example, in April of 2014 CVE-2014-0160 (http://web.nvd.nist.gov/view/vuln/detail?vulnId = CVE-2014-0160) was released, detailing a serious flaw in OpenSSL that could allow a malicious actor to obtain sensitive information from even SSL-encrypted communication. This flaw became known as the Heartbleed Bug. This was a wide-ranging and serious threat that potentially impacted thousands of information technology and security vendors, not to mention every Internet user. By working together to understand the nature of the threat the members of the IT-ISAC were able to improve the security of all members and, in turn, offer more effective protection for the entire Internet.

Another great example of the effectiveness of this type of sharing improving security for everyone is with the Industrial Control Systems (ICS)-ISAC (http://ics-isac.org). The ICS-ISAC is responsible for the security of the nations critical infrastructure. Unlike vertical ISACs, such as the FS-ISAC, the ICS-ISAC is a horizontal ISAC in that it works with organizations across a wide range of sectors. This cross-sector reach allows the ICS-ISAC CSIRT to communicate with many vendors across many industries to share immediate threats that may impact all of those sectors. As expected, membership in the ICS-ISAC is varied. Some of the members include Palo Alto, Cisco, the American Red Cross, New York Power Authority, Internet Systems Consortium (ISC), American Electric Power and Emerson.

To ensure effective security across such a wide range of vendors and industries the ICS-ISAC has created a guide for improving security in their networks. The guide is called the Situational Awareness Reference Architecture (SARA). SARA consists of four parts: Identity, Inventory, Activity, and Sharing. Essentially, by gathering a better understanding of an organization's goals, assets, and risks (Identity) and collecting information about the systems in use throughout the organization (inventory) and understanding who/what those systems have talked to and are talking to (activity) and gathering data from internal and external sources about the activity going on within the network (sharing) an organization can improve situational awareness.

When an organization improves situational awareness it also improves security posture and responsiveness to new security incidents.

SARA is a powerful framework and one worth investigating for organizations just experimenting with building out an intelligence-led security program.

Another very effective ISAC is the National Healthcare (NH) ISAC (http://www.nhisac.org/). The NH-ISAC is responsible for sharing cyber security information with a large number of constituencies within the healthcare sector, with the stated goal of moving members from a reactive security stance to a proactive one. Members of the NH-ISAC include healthcare providers, insurance companies, pharmaceutical companies, health information exchanges, technology companies support the healthcare industry, and many more organizations.

The NH-ISAC runs a 24×7 CSIRT known as the Global Situational Awareness Center (GSAC). The GSAC is responsible for processing security event information from NH-ISAC members or liaison organizations, providing incident response, and producing actionable finished intelligence to all members. The core of that communication is the Threat Information Sharing (TIS) Portal, which operates using the Lockheed Martin Cyber Kill Chain™ model mentioned in chapter 3.

The Multi-State (MS) ISAC (http://msisac.cisecurity.org/) is another effective ISAC that provide enormous value to its members. The MS-ISAC was founded in 2003 and serves state, local, tribal, and territorial (SLTT) governments. As with other ISACs, the MS-ISAC operates a 24×7 CSIRT. The MS-ISAC CSIRT assists members with breeches, malware analysis and forensics investigations. The MS-ISAC also collects security data from member organizations on a regular basis, which allows it to spots trends impacting SLTT governments and can relay that information to it members.

Because of its relationship with law enforcement and the security data it is collecting from its members, the MS-ISAC is often able to proactively notify its members when they have been compromised. For example, a compromised host in the State of Mississippi is being used as a redirector to launch an attack against infrastructure in the State of Hawaii. The MS-ISAC has several points in the attack where it may spot the attack, trace it back to Mississippi and notify the security team there. Above and beyond notification, if the State of Mississippi is a member, the MS-ISAC CSIRT team can assist with clean up and disseminate information from the attack to other members of the MS-ISAC.

The MS-ISAC offers additional services to its members such as cyber security advisories, daily and monthly newsletters, and both public and members-only webcasts.

Some industries have been faster than others to adopt the ISAC model. Two relatively new entries into the ISAC arena are the Retail-ISAC (http://www.rila.org/rcisc/RetailISAC/) and the Air Domain Intelligence Integration Center, for the aviation industry. Both organizations are modeling themselves heavily off of the FS-ISAC model. They will collect data from member organizations, serve as a liaison between government agencies and their members, provide support for member organization who suspect they have been breached and disseminate intelligence to all members in order to help improve security.

There are a number of benefits to joining a sector-specific ISAC. The ability to collaborate with organizations in the same industry in a secure and trusted manner is one. In addition, organizations that are members of an ISAC have the support of the ISAC's CSIRT and the knowledge of the government liaisons. The ISACs serve as a force multiplier, working with their industry counterparts to provide more effective security across the entire sector. The ISACs are also a rich source of both raw data and finished intelligence that can be combined with data from other sources to produce FINTEL within member organizations.

There are, of course, other ISACs that have not done nearly as good a job of sharing information with their members, or have even created any sort of cyber threat intelligence capability. Unfortunately, those ISACs are doing their members a serious disservice. An ISAC cannot solely focus on physical threats at this point, because even physical threats often have a cyber component. Hopefully, those few straggling ISACs will move toward providing more cyber threat intelligence sharing in the near future.

INTELLIGENCE-SHARING COMMUNITIES

CERTs are authoritative and generally provide one-way sharing of information that is broadly applicable. ISACs are sector-specific and more collaborative, providing much more focused data. Sometimes, even that focus is not enough. A security analyst in one organization might have information that could be of immediate value to a security analyst in another organization, but the analyst doesn't have an easy way to share that information with just that other analyst.

That is where the concept of intelligence-sharing communities comes into play. Companies like ThreatConnect (http://www.threatconnect.com/) and Vorstack (www.vorstack.com), and projects like FS-ISAC's Soltra (www.soltra.com) have built-in platforms that not only allow organizations to manage cyber threat intelligence data, but also create trusted communities for immediate information sharing. Figure 8.1 displays a sample intelligence-sharing community.

Intelligence-sharing communities, in their simplest form, are ways to securely share information between analysts within an organization, sector, or across a group of trusted analysts. Most intelligence data today is shared via email, but email is an insecure mechanism. Imagine, for example, a suspected targeted attack in part of an organization's network. Security analysts need to be able to identify the attack and track down adversary. They also need to understand the tools being used in the attack and all of the indicators associated with the adversary. The security team, working with the incident response team, the networking, team, and the system administrators, needs to be able to coordinate information about the attack and the planned steps to protect the network. If the adversary is advanced enough, there is a good chance the adversary is reading all of the email communication between the teams and knows what they know and can stay ahead of the security team. Even if an adversary is not reading email, email distribution lists quickly become unwieldy

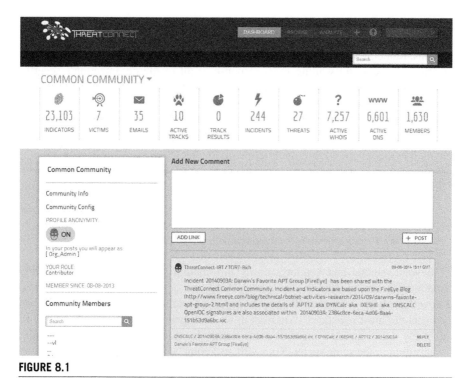

FIGURE 8.1

An example of an intelligence-sharing community from ThreatConnect.

as people change roles within an organization or more people request to be added to the distribution list. That unwieldiness can result in people who either no longer have a need to know, or never had a need to know becoming privy to sensitive information.

Instead, creating a non-email–based intelligence-sharing community on a secure platform will allow these teams to share information, and even develop a plan of counterattack to get the adversary removed from the network and prevent reinfection. By inviting only those individuals within the organization who will be part of the response, who have a need to know, dissemination of information can be kept at a minimum and this highly sensitive information can be better protected.

The above is an extreme example, but intelligence-sharing communities are useful for even routine information sharing within an organization. Organizations not only worry about the outside threat, but also the threat from well-meaning or malicious insiders. With email-based distribution of sensitive data that is used to form finished intelligence there is too much risk that the data will be leaked. Intelligence-sharing communities allow security teams to better restrict the flow of information and reduce the chances that sensitive data will be leaked.

Intelligence-sharing communities are not simply restricted to analysts within a single organization. These communities can be created to share information with trusted partners. Say a security analyst in an organization comes across a file the analyst suspects is malicious, but it is not showing up in any of the analyst's security systems. Rather than picking up the phone and calling three or four security vendors or emailing them and waiting for a response, if all of the organization's security vendors are part of a single intelligence-sharing community just for that organization, the analyst simply needs to submit all of the information to that community and the security vendors can each deliver what they know. The collected data could be compiled with other collected information and disseminated within the organization as FINTEL.

Some readers may be thinking that there is no way a security vendor would be willing to share proprietary information in a venue that other security vendors are monitoring. The nice thing about intelligence-sharing communities is that the flow of information can be restricted. In the example above, the analyst can post the question publicly, but the answers returned could all be private. This alleviates any concerns about one vendor seeing another vendor's proprietary information.

Beyond internal and vendor security information sharing, intelligence-sharing communities can be used to allow analysts at one organization to share information with analysts at another. This is the aspect of intelligence-sharing communities that gets the most resistance. Analysts in an intelligence-led security program will inevitably come across a piece of information that could be invaluable to another organization in the same sector. They will also come across a problem that someone else in that sector has seen and figured out how to protect against.

Of course, that information might be worth sharing at the ISAC level, but it often doesn't rise to that same level. Instead, having a secure platform that analysts from one organization can use to share information with trusted analysts from another organization makes sense. It helps to improve the security response of all organizations involved and increases the ability of analysts to track down real security threats.

The cyber security community is a small one and those within the cyber security community who are working in a cyber threat intelligence environment are even smaller. It is not unusual for a cyber threat intelligence analyst to jump from company to company every couple of years, all the while maintaining close ties to coworkers at previous companies. This is a long way of saying that the type of information sharing described above is already happening. Today, it happens over a beer or via email or text message. Creating a structured environment, like an intelligence-sharing community, helps organizations ensure that sensitive information is being handled properly a communication paths are controlled.

Intelligence sharing-communities are powerful tools in the hands of intelligence analysts. Intelligence-sharing communities offer secure, controlled communication between analysts. They can help analysts more effectively communicate with each other whether those analysts are within the same organization, partner organization or part of the same vertical.

CONCLUSION

Having trusted sources of security information, outside of security vendors, is important for understanding trends at the national, sector, and even internal levels. Organizations should, and many already do, rely on information from CERTs and ISACs to gain a better situational awareness around the threats that are facing their organization and how to prioritize those threats.

No organization has enough information to know about all of the threats targeting their network. By working with ISACs and intelligence-sharing communities analysts have the ability to reach out to others who are facing the same threats and collaborate to find a solution.

The more organizations within the same sector work together to improve security and share information the better protected the entire sector is.

REFERENCES

HSPD-7, 2003. Homeland security presidential directive 7 critical infrastructure identification, prioritization, and protection December 13, 2003. <http://www.dhs.gov/homeland-security-presidential-directive-7>. (accessed 16.08.14.).

PPD-63, 1998. Presidential Decision Directive–63, May 22, 1998. <http://fas.org/irp/offdocs/pdd/pdd-63.htm>. (accessed 16.08.14.).

Advanced intelligence capabilities

INFORMATION IN THIS CHAPTER:

- Malware analysis
- Honeypots
- Intrusion deception systems

INTRODUCTION

Moving an organization from "Whack-a-Mole" security to intelligence-led security is a big challenge in and of itself. Taking the next step and reaching out to peers through Information Sharing and Analysis Centers (ISACs) and community groups for the purposes of intelligence sharing is an even bigger challenge, and one for which most organizations are not ready. Beyond better information sharing, there are ways that an organization can improve its security and focus on intelligence.

Many of the tools discussed in this chapter are things that are normally outsourced to a trusted security partner. However, for some security teams it makes more sense to bring these capabilities in house. Generally speaking, the tools outlined in this chapter can produce valuable intelligence. But they also take time, sometimes significant amounts of time, from other security functions. Some of these tools can also introduce additional risk into an organization. Again, it is necessary for each organization to weigh the risk against the reward and determine what the right decision is for that organization.

This chapter has a slightly different format from the rest of the book. Each section has a subsection entitled "Why it is a bad idea." That doesn't necessarily mean that these ideas are bad, but that they are not appropriate for every network and not every organization is at a maturity level where they can take advantage of these ideas. In other words, proceed with caution.

MALWARE ANALYSIS

There are a number of tools – many of which were discussed earlier in this book – that automate the process of malware analysis. But, these tools generally conduct superficial analysis; they will conduct a cursory examination of a file and determine whether it is good or based on that high-level analysis.

However, some forms of malware are more complex and require more than a cursory review to determine exactly what it is doing. This is where having a malware lab can be very useful. A malware lab allows the security or incident response team to execute malware in a safe environment to understand what it does and what is needed to enable protection against the threat that particular piece of malware poses. If well executed, a malware lab can be a powerful tool for quickly understanding and protecting against new threats or unknown actors.

WHY IT IS A BAD IDEA

Before delving into the process of creating a malware lab it is important to step back and review why it is a bad idea. There are a number of negatives to running a malware lab in-house, including cost, lack of expertise, and the potential threat to the network that the security team is trying to protect. As interesting as it is, and it is very interesting, to dissect a piece of malware and discover the thinking that went into the development and delivery of the tool malware analysis is usually something that should be outsourced to a trusted security partner.

Managing a malware lab can be expensive. Even using the open source tools outlined later in this chapter, the man-hours and equipment costs alone can quickly eat into a security budget. That doesn't even take into account to cost of maintaining a unique network segment or, ideally, a completely isolated network with a separate network connection. Taking the "easy way" and selecting a commercial solution can be even more expensive, usually running hundreds of thousands of dollars for a solution that will provide the features and security precautions necessary to give enough piece of mind to assuage the concerns of leadership within the organization.

Even when budget is not a concern, lack of expertise is a serious concern that plagues many organizations. Knowing a programming language is not enough, it is also necessary to know how to program malware, to understand how the adversary thinks, the tools the adversary uses, and to be able to anticipate the precautions the adversary has taken to avoid detection. Malware analysis is more than just dropping a piece of malware into a sandbox and recording what happens. Reverse engineering malware starts long before the sandbox phase. The security engineer must get in the right mindset based on what operational, tactical, and strategic intelligence is available about the malware. Security engineers who are effective at malware analysis are rare and often expensive to hire. Even most organizations willing to hire security engineers specifically for their reverse engineering skills generally don't have enough unique, previously unseen, malware to keep that person busy full-time. Though, in some ways this is good, to be effective at reverse engineering of very targeted malware it is important to keep up on the latest trends in malware development. Adversaries are constantly finding new ways to ahead of current security tools, an effective malware analyst must spend a great deal of time studying and staying current on malware development trends.

This leads to a point that was made previously in this book. A number of security vendors have automated malware submission services. They allow their customers to upload a suspicious file which the vendor will analyze and provide a report back to the customer, offloading the work and allowing the customer's security team to focus on their core functions.

Finally, malware analysis presents a real danger to an organization. By definition, malware that is unique enough that it is not identified by any existing security is dangerous. Even if the malware is quickly identified and isolated, the simple act of transporting it from one system to another can cause problems. Copy it to a thumb drive? Did it leave an artifact on that thumb drive that can jump to another machine when it is plugged in next? Even if it is successfully transported, until it is analyzed how can a security team be sure that everything has been successfully captured until the malware is fully analyzed? Executing it in a sandbox? Does the malware behave differently in a sandbox environment versus a real machine? It is not uncommon for improperly designed and implemented malware labs to become the source of infection into the rest of the network.

SETTING UP A MALWARE LAB

Sometimes it makes more sense for an organization to set up its own malware lab, rather than outsourcing this function to a partner. There can be a number of reasons for this, but the most prominent seems to be that the organization is targeted by very specialized malware and it does not want information about that malware released to the world. Generally speaking, though definitely not always, when an organization shares suspected malware with a security vendor to analyze the vendor will release a report on the malware not only back to the original requestor but also the rest of that vendor's customers and sometimes to the rest of the Internet. Of course, releasing that information is simply good security practice, but it can alert a sophisticated adversary that their tool was discovered and, depending on how much the security vendor shares, its operation is blown. A second reason for to keep malware analysis in house is that, with the right setup, an internal malware analysis lab can provide a much faster turn-around time for distributing malware analysis. In the world of network security, speed is of the essence. If there are components of a piece of malware that were missed during the initial triage a slow response time from a security vendor can mean that the malware is spreading unchecked through an organization's network. In either of these cases, it might make sense for organizations with the right staffing and allocated budget to invest in building a malware lab in-house.

Once an organization has decided that a malware lab is a necessity, the next step is to decide the best way to go about setting up the lab. There are commercial solutions from companies such as FireEye (http://www.fireeye.com/), ThreatTrack Security (http://www.threattracksecurity.com/) and Joe Security (http://www.joesecurity.org) that provide self-contained sandbox solutions, which automate the analysis of malware on the local network or in the cloud. These solutions are plug-and-play: users simply drop the suspect file into a web interface and wait for a report that contains a reverse analysis of the malware. These solutions have the advantage of being self-contained and simple to use. The experts at these companies are fully aware of the latest tricks malware writers are using to circumvent analysis and they know how to circumvent the circumventions. Although these solutions can be effective, they are also expensive, both the initial cost and ongoing maintenance.

If an all-in-one solution is not an option, the next question is what type of malware lab does the organization want. The choices can range from using a few useful tools on a segmented, stand-along box dedicated only for malware analysis to building a full sandbox environment.

This point cannot be emphasized enough: Analyzing malware is inherently dangerous. If a malicious program is not detected by existing security tools, there is a good chance it is even more dangerous than originally thought. Proceed with caution.

Planning the network

The first step in building a malware analysis lab is planning the network that will host the lab. If it is a multi-node network, it should be isolated from the rest of the network – this can be done using virtual local area networks (VLANs) or even by putting the network into its own demilitarized zone (DMZ). If a single machine is going to be used, it should not be connected to the larger corporate network. In both instances serious consideration should be given to acquiring Internet connectivity that is separate from the rest of the network. With the proliferation of bot-focused black lists, it is very easy for a victim host to wind up on another organization's block list. The last thing anyone wants is for an organization's malware lab to land it on a watch list while conducting analysis. A separate concern is that the IP address calling to the command and control host from the malware lab will become a target. It is better if that IP address is not directly associated with the targeted organization.

The next consideration is the number and type of images that are needed to successfully analyze malware. A lot of consideration and planning needs to be done here, even in a single-machine environment, a number of nodes are necessary to effectively analyze modern malware.

Virtual machines versus cloning

Before discussing the types of machines needed for a malware lab it is necessary to wade into the debate over physical versus virtual machines. No malware lab should rely on permanently installed operating systems; that is a recipe for disaster. However, there are different ways to load images onto the lab systems. The most common way is to use virtualization systems such as products from VMWare, Microsoft, and Parallels. These tools are great because they allow multiple systems to run simultaneously on the same machine. This means that malware analyst can create a replica of the entire network including Active Directory Server, File Server, DNS Server, Web Server, and victim machines on a single – albeit powerful – machine. Virtual machines are also useful from the perspective of being easy to bring them up and tear them down, this is especially important when trying to determine how a tested malware behaves on different versions of Microsoft Windows, or even the same version with different patch levels.

Of course, there are downsides to using a virtual machine environment. One of the biggest problems is that malware developers are aware of the techniques used to analyze their code. Some malware developers will include routines in their code that look for virtual platforms, and will either not execute or behave differently in those virtual platforms. Another tactic of malware developers who see that their code is being executed within a virtual environment is to try to attack the hypervisor – the host operating system. This is one of the reasons why running on an isolated network is so critical, the last thing a malware analyst wants is to have the test system compromised and used to infect the rest of the network. Finally, if an attack is truly targeted, intended for a specific individual, then it may not run in a virtual environment unless that environment perfectly mirrors the intended target's machine. While this last condition is rare, it is not unheard of and needs to be taken into account when deciding how to build out a malware lab.

The second way to create images is by using cloning tools such as Symantec Ghost or Acronis True Image. These tools have the advantage of being faster to install than a traditional operating system installation, and they allow malware analysts to build out systems that have all the necessary tools already installed. When a new piece of malware needs to be analyzed the researcher simply builds a system, or multiple system, using the stored images and copies it to the victim machine. After the analysis is complete, delete the image from the computer and secure delete the hard drive. The security team is still able to respond quickly to suspected malware, while dealing with some of the problem associated with using virtual machines. Cloning tools also have the advantage of being able to be used on the victim machine itself. If the security team suspects a specific machine has been targeted, simply clone it and bring it back up in the malware lab. This allows for better contextual malware analysis of the malware because all of the original logs from the attack will still be present (Web sites visited, attachments opened, etc). Just as with other types of intelligence, malware analysis cannot exist in a vacuum. Understanding the tactical and the strategic intelligence associated with the malware is just as important as understanding the operational, if a security team is going to prevent further infection within the network.

There are, of course, downsides to using image clones within a malware lab. Managing cloned images takes more time and effort. This can be especially true when it comes to keeping them updated so that they properly mirror the systems in use on the network. Using image clones in a malware lab also requires a more complex closed network. Even with cloned images server infrastructure is necessary to see what a piece of malware does when it is allowed to run wild. For example, if the observed malware has an exploit to attack the Active Directory service in a network, the only way to find out for sure is for there to be an Active Directory server there for it to attack. That does not mean that every possible service/application that can be exploited should exist in the malware lab, but the essential services that effectively mirror what is in the larger network should be represented – especially in cases where the security team is not sure of all the systems impacted by the initial breach. The setup time for a malware lab running cloned systems is also longer. While building a system from a clone is a faster than installing from scratch, it is still not as fast a simply starting up a virtual image. Finally, the possibility exists that the malware can jump from the cloned operating system to the machine on which it is running. Some malware contains the ability to embed itself in the Basic Input/Output System (BIOS) of the underlying system. When the BIOS is infected, it will continue to infect the system every time a new cloned image is installed. Which is why it is critical to not only secure erase the hard drive after each use, but also to make sure the BIOS is reset and clean.

Getting the malware to the lab

Whichever method is used to set up a malware lab, the next decision that needs to be made is how to get sample data to the lab. Remember that the malware lab, however it is ultimately set up, should never be able to talk back to the organization's network. Generally, the malware network is considered a dirty network, while the organization's network is considered a clean network.[1] The trick is to devise a way to get the data safely from the clean network to the dirty network in a manner that does not put other assets in the clean network at risk.

Malware labs that are using cloning systems will simply clone the infected system to a hard drive that is only used for this purpose and can walk that hard drive to the dirty network to load it up. Similarly, with virtualized networks it is possible to isolate the malware and copy it to a portable drive – again one that is only used for this purpose and secure erased afterwards – which can be walked over to the dirty network. These methods are great for organizations that are contained within the same building or group of buildings, but they don't work well for organizations that are spread out around the world.

Even the largest organizations with a large security staff are only going to have one malware lab, so in cases where there are remote breaches that require malware analysis there are limited options. At the risk of stopping productivity for an extended period of time the infected machine or laptop can be shipped to the malware lab for analysis. Alternatively, the security team can build a one-way throw from the clean network to the dirty network. A one-way throw is a method of transferring data that allows one network to speak to another network, but the second network cannot initiate communication back to the first network. This communication is usually done over an SSH (secure socket shell) or an HTTPS (Hypertext Transfer Protocol Secure) connection to ensure encrypted end-to-end traffic. The one-way throw is especially useful for passing single files such as PDF files or Microsoft Word documents that are suspected of containing embedded Trojans.

Whichever method makes sense for an organization to transfer files from the clean network to the dirty network it is important to have a security plan built around it. The security plan will clearly define what is allowed and not allowed for transport and who is authorized to load files from the clean network to the dirty network.

---

[1]Though, realistically, no network of any size is truly clean.

Malware tools

Every malware analyst has a favorite set of tools the analyst likes to use to pick apart malware and understand what it does. This section lists a small subset of those tools, and is not intended to be comprehensive. A security researcher who is interested in learning more about malware analysis should play around with multiple types of the tools to understand how they work and what type of intelligence can be gathered from each tool.

Just as someone who wants to become proficient at picking locks has a to invest in a good lock pick kit as well as a number of different locks to practice, it is a good idea to practice malware analysis on several different types of malware that have already been fully analyzed.

One way to do this is to identify a file that has been quarantined by the organization's endpoint protection system, take a hash of that file, and run the hash through an online automated threat detection system such as ThreatExpert (http://www.threatexpert.com/).

ThreatExpert will provide a full analysis that can be compared against the analysis performed locally to see what matches and what doesn't. The more often this is done the better the ability of the security team to conduct malware analysis.

Before conducting the actual malware analysis it is important to catalogue the malware. Remember that malware analysis is not conducted for the sake of analyzing malware. Instead, the goal is to enhance the security posture of the organization by providing intelligence around a new, or at least previously unseen, threat. Start by hashing the file using a tool like md5deep. A cryptographic hash of the file, usually in MD5 or SHA256 formats, creates a fingerprint that can be checked against other sources and also loaded into local security systems like Blue Coat or FireEye to provide immediate protection to the rest of the network. That file hash should also be associated with any other indicators that are known from the initial attack. For example, if it was a spear-phishing attack the from address, time of delivery, subject like, IP address of the mail relay server, and any URL or file name included in the email should now all be tied to that hash. Connecting the dots like this will allow the organization to better understand the tactical and operational threat, even if the strategic threat is still unknown.

In addition to recording the indicators from the victim system it is also useful to analyze the memory of the system for any artifacts related to the malware (this needs to be done before the system reboots). Tools like Mandiant's Memoryze pull artifacts from the memory of the victim machine that can be associated with the other indicators discovered during the malware analysis process.

Now comes the fun part, actually analyzing the malware! Before getting to the actual code a malware researcher has to determine what type of packer was used on the malware. A packer is a program that compresses an executable and, especially in the case of malware, adds an additional layer encryption to avoid reverse engineering and detection by antivirus programs. Packing an executable is not inherently a bad thing; in fact, most developers use a packer like UPX to reduce the size of their executable programs or scripts.

When it is used to protect malware, packing creates all sorts of problems for reverse engineering. Without knowing which packer was used it is extremely challenging to unpack the malware to get to the actual code. Fortunately, there are tools that help malware analysts determine which packing tool was used. Kaspersky and other antivirus programs have built in packer detectors and usually have command line tools that will help malware engineers peel that first layer. Alternatively, there are stand-alone tools like Detect It Easy that maintain signatures of the most common packing tools use by malware developers and can be checked against an unknown piece of malware.

Once a piece of malware has been successfully unpacked, don't be afraid to examine the strings. There is a lot of valuable data, not always directly related to the code, which can be uncovered from within the strings. For example what language are the comments in? Are there any strings that tie the code to a particular programmer (it is amazing the number of times programs strings have revealed things like: c:\users\[Malware Developer's Name]\projects\[Malware Name]). Reviewing the strings can be very helpful for finding information about the person who wrote the program.

Strings are also useful for finding hard-coded information about the command and control (C&C) structure inside the malware. If there is a specific list of IP addresses or domains to which the malware is supposed to call back, those will often be embedded in the code.

Finally, it is time to disassemble the software. By far, the most common tool a malware analyst uses for this task is Hey-Rays IDA Pro. IDA is an Interactive DisAssembler that allows a program to execute while tracking the calls the program makes. IDA Pro allows malware researchers to map out exactly what a program is doing, programmatically, as it executes and presents a full report to the analyst for review. It enables malware analysts to reverse engineer a piece of malware without actually seeing the assembly code.

Using these tools, or tools similar to them, will provide a view of how the program operates but it does not always provide the full picture. Malware analysts must also record the effect on the system and the surrounding network when malware executes.

System tools

To fully understand the effect a piece of malware has on a system, it is necessary to understand the changes that the malware makes to the system. To do that, the security team must first have a baseline of what the system looks like. This may sound obvious, but too many security teams forget this step, so it is worthy of a reminder.

One of the basic things that a malware analyzer needs to do is monitor changes to the processes and the registry that are made by the malware. Microsoft Sysinternals Process Monitor tool does an excellent job of tracking those changes. With the right filters Process Monitor has the ability to quickly identify not only new processes but also changes to already running processes. The latter is important when reverse engineering malware that injects itself into other processes. Process Monitor also provides a list of the process owners, so the malware researcher can determine if the malware is running using user privileges or attempting to run using administrative privileges. Process monitor also tracks new files installed or copied to the system. Malware will often try to install several components when it is first unpacked, knowing all of the file names (and hashing those files) helps provide additional information that the security team can use to protect the rest of the network.

Malware does not just impact the local system it has an impact on the rest of the network. Which is why, in addition to a system analyzer, it is important to have something to analyze network traffic. A very common network analyzer is Wireshark. Wireshark will allow a malware analyst to understand not just where the malware is trying to communicate, but also what that communication looks like. It can also monitor any internal network scanning to try to understand how malware attempts to replicate itself within the network.

This leads to one of the biggest conundrums that malware analysts face: should the malware be allowed to reach the C&C host? To this point, a lot of data has been gathered: file hashes for the malware, domains and IP addresses used for communication, Registry changes, system process names, types of scanning the malware does, and what the communication with the C&C host looks like. Actually allowing the malware to reach the host can provide even more information. For example, there is generally no operation-specific tasking embedded in the malware, that occurs after successful call out to the C&C host. Knowing what the operational tasking for the malware can tell an organization a lot about the adversary behind the malware and start to fill in additional gaps. Allowing the malware to reach the C&C host can also result in additional tools being downloaded onto the "victim" system and it might even result in a direct connection to the adversary as he tries to gain direct control of the compromised system. From an intelligence perspective, this can be extremely useful information.

The downside to allowing access like that is that the compromised system can also be used as a redirector to launch attacks against other systems. Although sophisticated malware is generally the sign of an advanced attacker, it could also be a spammer who happens to have written a tool that the antivirus vendors have not seen yet. Even if it is only for a short while, an organization's malware lab could potentially be turned into a spam relay. Careful consideration has to be given to both scenarios and the risks need to be clearly understood and communicated within the organization.

Sandbox

There are some systems that are prebuilt with all of the tools needed for malware analysis in place, all the researcher has to do is drop the malware into the system and let it run. These are known as sandboxes. In many ways they are more efficient than using a number of different tools, they are also more automated. For organizations that do analyze a lot of malware, a sandbox makes more sense because it will significantly improve the efficiency of malware analysis.

Probably the most well-known and widely used sandbox is Cuckoo (http://www.cuckoosandbox.org). Cuckoo is fully self-contained malware analyzer that records all Windows calls, any files that are created during the malware installation, a memory dump, a recording of any attempts at network communication, and any desktop screenshots. It not only records all of that information it also produces a report, in a variety of formats, that contains the information. This makes the data collected easy to read and disseminate.

An alternative for organizations that prefer an all-Windows environment is Sanboxie (http://www.sandboxie.com) combined with Buster (http://bsa.isoftware.nl). Sanboxie is different in that rather than turn the entire system into a sandbox, it runs each application on the system within its own sandbox. This allows Sanboxie to intercept any calls the application makes to the system and limits any damage to the application itself. If an attacker manages to exploit the user's web browser, the attacker cannot use that access to gain access to the rest of the system. By incorporating Buster into Sandboxie a security team is able to track the changes made to those applications, providing a better understanding of what the malware does and the changes it makes to the system on which it is installed.

Turning data into intelligence

The final step of the malware analysis process is to turn the data collected into actionable intelligence. Using the intelligence pyramid, the data collected can be divided into potential strategic, tactical, and operational intelligence and compared to data collected from other sources. The data needs to be written up in a consistent and complete manner that can be delivered into a central analysis platform and converted into finished intelligence (FINTEL) to be disseminated into the organization.

The type of data that should be included in the final malware analysis report should include things like file name with associated hashes; method of delivery; indicators from the delivery including email addresses or Web sites; Registry entries; process names; C&C host address; observations from the code review; sample of the C&C traffic; and types of scanning the malware does. These are just some examples of data that should be included; there are many more indictors that could be useful. Again, it is important that a standardized list is developed within the organization and that list is consistently applied and readable by the tools analysts use.

How does this information get turned into intelligence? By matching indictors uncovered during the malware analysis process with indicators from other systems on the network, or other analyst tools. For example, the Whois information from the C&C domain may match the Whois information from a domain used in another attack that was tied to a specific adversary. Another example could be that the communication pattern between the malware and the C&C host may have been observed by the Lancope Stealthwatch installation or by the Intrusion Detection System (IDS). Correlating data from malware analysis, especially if the malware is presently unknown, can produce intelligence that helps to improve the security of the larger organization.

Of course, malware analysis should not stop there. Unless there is sensitive information uncovered during the malware analysis process, the report should be shared with other organizations that could benefit from understanding the threat. Whether that sharing is through a member ISAC or through a trusted security vendor by disseminating a partial version of the FINTEL, an organization may be able to help other organizations prevent an attack or uncover an ongoing breach.

HONEYPOTS

Honeypots and honeynets are tools designed to improve network security by positioning systems, or entire networks, that appear to be vulnerable to known attacks in places where the attackers are looking. The systems are not always actually vulnerable to the attacks. Instead, they help security teams better understand the types of attacks the adversaries are using against the organization by collecting data on the attacks, including the exploits used, and delivering that data to the security team.

In their book, *Offensive Countermeasures: The Art of Active Defense,* Strand, Asadoorian, Robish, and Donnelly (2013) define a honeypot as:

> *"…any object within your environment that is tempting for malicious attackers to interact with. It should be noted that honeypot technology can be anything, not just systems. At the same time, it should never be interacted with."*

WHY IT IS A BAD IDEA

Honeypots and honeynets are bad idea because, in many ways, they have outlived their usefulness. In the early 2000s, honeypots were more important because most successful attacks against networks occurred at the edge. That is not the case anymore; successful attacks today start inside the network via an email or someone clicking a link. It is highly unlikely that a honeypot sitting in the DMZ of an organization's network is going to see anything new or interesting in the way of attacks. The current state of affairs in network security belies the arguments that many honeypot proponents make: Honeypots help capture zero-day exploits. By all accounts most attackers are not using zero-day exploits, even if they have them. Most attackers use older exploits against unpatched systems, because those exploits work. Why bother to burn a new exploit against a network, when one that has been around for a couple of years will still work?

The rise of vulnerability-and-exploitation–type data feeds also has limited the effectiveness of honeypots in some ways. Any exploits being used against a specific network have undoubtedly been used against other networks and seen more recently by the security company offering the vulnerability-and-exploitation service. Their knowledge very likely trumps any knowledge gained from the local honeypot, because they can often correlate their information against vertical data and possibly adversary data to present not only that the exploit exists but which groups are using it who are they targeting.

The counterargument to this is that there are still a lot of attacks that occur at the edge. This is trueish; there is a lot of attacker activity occurring at the edge, networks are constantly being scanned, and automated tools are constantly launching attacks at Web servers, mail servers, and anything else with an IP address in the DMZ. Very few of those attacks are successful because organizations today, do a much better job of securing the perimeter. What this means is that a honeypot placed in the DMZ will most likely be collecting data on thousands of scans and other low-level attacks each day. Creating more work for the analysts that need to review the data with very little positive results.

The other danger posed by honeypots is that they often run on potentially vulnerable systems. So, while the honeypot is pretending to be a vulnerable web server it may in fact be running a vulnerable FTP server or a vulnerable remote desktop solution. A vulnerable honeypot can serve as a point of entry, or at the very least a redirector, into the target network actually making the job of the adversary easier.

For further proof that most organizations think adopting honeypot technology is a bad simply look at the commercial market. Ten years ago almost every large security vendor offered a commercial honeypot solution. Today, none of them do. There are still commercial solutions available, but they tend to be from boutique security firms that specialize in honeypots. Some large security vendors do offer what are, in effect, honeypots to their clients to monitor traffic, but those solutions tend to be fully managed by the security vendor with the customer having little insight into the collected data.

POSITIONING A HONEYPOT

While it is true that honeypots within the DMZ have become less effective over the years, there is still an area where honeypots can be useful: inside the network. In the end the effectiveness of a honeypot is all about where it sits within the network. Given the nature of today's attack activity, a DMZ-based honeypot may not make sense, but several of them positioned throughout the network might make a lot of sense.

The bad news is positioning honeypots inside a network is basically an acknowledgement that the network has been breached or will be breached at some point. The good news is most likely a network of any size has most likely already been breached; so using honeypots is simply a reflection of reality.

Using honeypots inside the network means changing the expectations for the honeypots somewhat. A honeypot in the DMZ is like a canary in the mine, it is an early warning that something bad is going to happen to the network and action must be taken. A honeypot inside the network is more like instant replay: here is what happened, now take steps to keep it from happening again or getting worse.

In the attack chain model outlined in Chapter 3 (see p. 0000) after a target network is successfully exploited the attacker begins to explore the network looking for the information necessary to complete the attacker's mission. Placing the right honeypots with the right lures inside the places within the network can serve as an alert the security team that a network user has been compromised.

For a honeypot to be effective in this scenario it must appear to be something that is going to be attractive to an adversary. It also must have the ability to log and deliver information about connections to the honeypot in a timely manner to the security team. Finally, the honeypot must not be something that is going to see regular traffic from legitimate users on the network. For example, placing a honeypot on the network with the machine name [FILESERVER] will absolutely attract any attackers on the network, but it will also most likely draw traffic from real users looking for files.

Deployed correctly, honeypots can also be a useful tool for collecting adversary attribution information. A well-placed honeypot, with the right lure, can often force an adversary to abandon the adversary's redirector and gain direct access to the machine. The source IP address can be very valuable in determining who is really behind the attack.

CREATING A PLAN

Honeypots should never be deployed in a network in an ad-hoc manner. Just as with any other security platform they need to be deployed as part of a larger security plan. Honeypots, especially, should have leadership approval for deploying – not only does this protect the security team it also forces them to create and justify a detailed deployment plan. Being able to justify the deployment and explain the security goals of the honeypot deployment are important because there will undoubtedly be a lot of pushback from leadership who can see honeypots as nothing but a "science experiment" or, worse, a liability within the organization.

The planning of the honeypot deployment should align with the missions of the organization and should be optimized to collect data that is going to lead to the greatest amount of FINTEL production. Some of the questions that need to be asked are: What are the most valuable assets in the organization? What systems contain those assets? How would an adversary gain access to those systems? Questions like these will help narrow the focus of the honeypot deployment. These questions will also help determine what types of honeypots to deploy.

Honeypot deployment planning should also take into consideration not only geographic considerations, but business demographic disbursement, and proximity to actual servers.

TYPES OF HONEYPOTS

Most people are familiar with honeypots masquerading as vulnerable servers, but there is actually a wide range of honeypots. Traditionally, honeypots have been divided into two types: low-interaction and high-interaction honeypots. A low-interaction honeypot simply captures connection attempts and alerts the security team an intrusion has been attempted. A high-interaction honeypot, on the other hand, allows attackers to compromise and gain access to the system. The honeypot then monitors the attacker and records all activity that occurs on the machine. Although high-interaction honeypots can provide a wealth of information, they also can introduce additional risk into the network.

Those definitions are somewhat limiting as there are a range of different types of honeypots that can be deployed. In fact, the more varied the deployment of honeypots throughout the network, the more effective they are at attracting attackers and alerting the security team to breaches in the network. Now, to do that effectively, the honeypots must all talk to a central repository. Just as with everything else discussed throughout the book, it does not matter how valuable the data collected is, it doesn't improve the security of the organization if it cannot be quickly accessed and analyzed by the security team.

Another type of honeypot is a honeytoken. A honeytoken is an artifact that is designed to be attractive to an attacker exfiltrating data from a network, but not accessed by anyone who is a legitimate user of the network. A honeytoken is a form of honeypot, but instead of a server, a honeytoken is a file, login credentials, database table (sometimes referred to as a honeytable), credit card information, or anything else that looks like a real file but is not. That is the critical part of a honeytoken–it has to accurately reflect what the attacker would expect to find on the network, but not be real data. So, an Excel spreadsheet that is named "Credit_Card_Numbers_with_CVV_Codes.xlsx" should contain numbers that look like real credit card numbers at a cursory glance. Similarly, a file labeled "passwords.txt" should contain what look like real account names (but not real account names) associated with bad passwords. The point is to make the data too attractive to resist for an attacker, while at the same time creating security notifications when the data is accessed or used. In the case of the bad passwords, if they are associated with fake users an alert should be generated every time someone tries to log into a system with the bad username.

Honeytokens are especially common in database security. There are two main reasons for this. The first is that most organizations keep some of their most sensitive data within their databases, so every countermeasure needs to be taken in order to protect the data. The second reason is that it is easy to track queries to a database. A fake table created specifically to track queries by malicious actors generates a log every time it is queried. This gives the security team instant information about which IP address the query originated from and the username that was used to access the database, simplifying the incident response. It may not be that user initiating the query, but it does provide a place to start the investigation.

Another area where honeytokens can be very helpful is as an added layer of security for a Web server. While most attacks against servers in the DMZ are ineffective, attacks on Web servers are still a problem for organizations. In fact, Zone-H maintains an active list of defaced Web sites (http://www.zone-h.org/archive), which seems to be over time. By planting honeytokens in areas that attackers look for data, but regular site visitors do not, such as the robots.txt file or in subdirectories, it is possible to not only notify security teams that someone is conducting reconnaissance on the Web site, but perhaps put a halt to the attack. The one caution with using honeytokens on a Web server is that there are likely hundreds or thousands of automated tools scanning an organization's Web site every day. It is important to place the honeytokens in a way that they do not generate hundreds of alerts each day – otherwise they will wind up being ignored and be a less-than-effective security measure.

CHOOSING A HONEYPOT

How does an organization determine which honeypots are right for them? One of the best ways to do get familiar with honeypots is to spend time with the honeypot community. The Honeynet Project (https://www.honeynet.org) is the most vibrant and active honeypot community on the Internet. It is a great place to go to find out which tools work well for their members as well as learn about new tools. Getting involved in the Honeynet Project community is a great way to get a deeper understanding of honeypot projects, play around with the various honeypots available and determine the best way to set up a network of honeypots.

There are some specific tools that are worth looking at to get started, with the caveat that sometimes honeypot projects gain a lot of steam and then fade away; four years from now this list may look very different.

A simple way to get started is with HoneyBOT from Atomic Software Solutions (http://www.atomicsoftwaresolutions.com). HoneyBOT is a Windows-based honeypot that can be installed and set up in a few minutes. It gives users the ability to create a simple, low-interaction to medium-interaction honeypot that monitors connections on ports and services and can report connections via syslog to a centralized collection point. KFSensor, by Key Focus (http://www.keyfocus.net/kfsensor/), is a more advanced honeypot that is low interaction. In addition to port monitoring, KFSensor allows a security team can adjust banners, so it can mirror non-Windows daemons. It also allows custom services to be written and installed as plugins.

Security teams ready to move to the next level in honeypots can look at The Active Defense Harbinger Distribution (ADHD) (http://sourceforge.net/projects/adhd/). ADHD is an Ubuntu distribution (full ISO) that contains a number of tools used to create honeypots and honeytokens. The distribution was developed by several of the authors of *Offensive Countermeasures: The Art of Active Defense* (Strand et al, 2013). Because ADHD is an ISO designed to be run from CD/thumb drive, it is fun to play with the tools without having to necessarily install anything.

There are also specialty projects that are worth investigating, such as the Google Hack Honeypot (GHH) (http://ghh.sourceforge.net). GHH is a project that has not been updated in a while, but the premise is interesting. It looks at the common tactics of attackers who use search engines for reconnaissance and plants honeytokens on the target Web site that will provide bad information to the attacker while not interfering at all with real search engine traffic or real users traffic.

Regardless of the honeypots chosen for deployment in the network, it is important to ensure that they are being continuously monitored. A honeypot not being monitored is a security risk, not just to the system on which it is deployed but also to the entire network. Once again, it is also important to emphasize that any solution that is deployed should have a way to send logs to a centralized logging system, and those honeypots and honeytokens should be clearly identified in that system. Correlating the logs against other systems in the network is important for ultimately producing intelligence. But, the fact that the data is coming from a properly deployed honeypot should raise the severity of that data in producing FINTEL.

INTRUSION DECEPTION

People who develop malware and attack networks make the cost of doing business more expensive. They do this by forcing organizations to incur additional costs, in both equipment and employees, to protect their network. Adversaries also increase the cost of doing business by stealing information and leaking it to competing organizations or governments. These organizations then use the information to make cheaper versions of the target organization's product, interfere with merger and acquisition plans, disrupt treaty negotiations, or any of hundreds of other ways that they can make things difficult for the target organization. The idea behind intrusion deception tools is to switch this up and make attacking the target organization more expensive for the attackers.

Intrusion deception tools are used to confuse and deceive attackers. They are not tools designed to "hack back" against the adversary, at least, not in the sense of launching an offensive network attack against the adversary. In fact, in almost all cases, "hacking back is a bad idea and not recommended.

That being said, intrusion deception is a form hacking in the truest sense – the idea is to anticipate what adversaries are going to be looking for and make it more difficult for those adversaries to get at that data, using a number of different techniques. Intrusion deception can be a powerful tool and can help protect a network's assets even when it has been compromised.

WHY IT IS A BAD IDEA

Most security teams are already overwhelmed with incidents; adding a new capability is out of the question. Not to mention that to engage in effective intrusion deception the security team may need a deep understanding of areas of the business that are not their mainstay. There is a good chance that a security analyst does not understand how to read blueprints, the topology of the organization's Web site, or even know how to make fake credit card information. Alternatively, the people within the organization that might be able to do that are undoubtedly extremely busy themselves, and don't have time to assist in producing and maintaining the necessary information for a good intrusion deception campaign.

Intrusion deception can also pose significant risk to an organization. A false positive – handing fake information to a legitimate user with a legitimate need for it – might result in millions of dollars of lost revenue, or worse. Meanwhile, there is no guarantee that the attackers will fall for the fake information. If the attackers are not deceived then a lot of time, effort, and money will be wasted.

HOW INTRUSION DECEPTION WORKS

There are a number of different ways to use intrusion deception against an adversary depending on the level of sophistication and the risk profile of the organization. For the most part, though, intrusion deception involves taking honeytokens to the next level. Where honeytokens are simply meant to fool attackers and waste time, intrusion deception techniques are meant to taint their entire operation. However, intrusion deception techniques, like honeypots, assume that an organization is either in the process of or has already been breached.

Many of these intrusion deception systems will sit outside of the system that is being targeted by the attackers. For example, Juniper Networks' WebApp Secure (formerly known as Mykonos) monitors activity occurring on a Web server and when it detects activity that appears to be malicious it will intervene. This intervention can take the form of throwing up a Captcha box that the attacker must fill out before the attacker can proceed, or slowing down the connection from the suspect IP address, or even forcing the attacker to click on a dialogue box before going from page to page. WebApp Secure (http://www.juniper.net/us/en/products-services/security/webapp-secure/) differs from traditional Web server–based honeytokens in that it is adaptive to its surroundings – it changes tactics depending on what it observes the attacker doing.

In addition to slowing down, and hopefully thwarting, the attack this type of intrusion deception system forces the attacker to reach deeper into the attacker's "bag of tricks" as the operation becomes more difficult. Understanding the different tools used helps to build a profile a profile of the adversary that can be checked against other exploitation attempts.

Tools like Deceptos are another example of intrusion deception in which they replace information targeted by the adversary with similar, but not inaccurate information. A honeytoken file is one that is meant to look attractive to an attacker, but is really meant to distract them from the real files. File-based intrusion deception systems assume the attacker has found the real file and when the attacker attempts to exfiltrate the file these systems replace it with a similar, but slightly altered file.

Of course, these systems are not limited to files; database queries and other sources of information can also be replaced. The intrusion deception system looks for activity that is indicative of malicious behavior, whether that is a malicious outsider or insider, and based on that activity determine whether to deliver the real or the fake file as it is requested.

Generally, this type of deception is something that won't be noticed for weeks or months giving the security team plenty of time to take advantage of the notification from the intrusion deception system to clean the compromised machines. Now, even if the adversary eventually realizes they have collected bad information they will need to gain access to the network again and start the process all over.

By using these, and other, intrusion deception techniques a security team can continue to protect the assets of the network even when a breach has occurred. Making things difficult for an adversary by increasing their cost of doing business helps to keep the network secure.

CONCLUSION

The techniques discussed in this chapter can help to provide additional data that leads to better intelligence about the adversaries targeting a network. Ultimately, the data collected from these systems can improve the security of the network. That being said, they are not a fundamental part of an intelligence-led security program. The fundamentals of an intelligence-led security program should be in place before investing in the tools outlined in this chapter.

REFERENCE

Strand, J., Asadoorian, P., Robish, E., Donnelly, B., 2013. Offensive Countermeasures: The Art of Active Defense. Amazon Digital Services. Seattle, WA, p. 59.

Index

Printed and bound by CPI Group (UK) Ltd, Croydon, CR0 4YY

03/10/2024

01040324-0018